Waves of Stardust

All rights reserved; no part of this book may be reproduced, stored in a retrieval system, or transmitted, in any form or by any means, without the prior permission in writing from the publisher, nor be otherwise circulated in any form of binding or cover other than that in which it is published and without a similar condition including this condition being imposed on the subsequent purchaser.

First published in Great Britain in 2022 by Turqoise Quill Press
an imprint of Not From This Planet

Copyright © 2022 by Elizabeth Lockwood
Cover Illustration by Lucja Fratczak-Kay
Illustrations by Elizabeth Lockwood
Formatting by The Amethyst Angel

ISBN: 978-1-912257-65-2

The moral right of the author has been asserted.

First Edition

Waves of Stardust

poetry & illustrations
by
elizabeth lockwood

also by
elizabeth lockwood

LITTLE SOMETHING

for osian joseph lockwood

our time together was short
but our love will never end

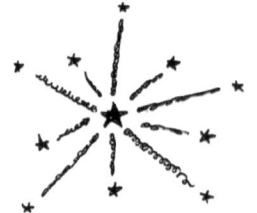

The Blessing

Brightly lit, luminous
Dust sifts down
Released from the brightest star
To where all blossoms burgeon and bloom
In watchful, waitful, wakeful wombs
Steadfast in the ordinary
Living the extraordinary
The glory, the beauty
The blessing
A new person
Scattering magic
Simmering dreams
Bringing love
As a gift
To the world

another sun rises

A week ago in the soft summer dawns
I found out I was pregnant
Unreal in the rising of the sun
Yet real in the plastic and chemical lines.
Shaking off the judgment
Leaves a cold feeling.
Why would they want another child?
They have three already
She's had three c-sections, you know
A fourth section – at her age?
My womb. The surgery.
1 in 4?
But I've already been 1 in 4
Lost the ones that preceded the three
They don't get it
They can't see
Trust like a tightrope walker
Balance like your life depends on it
But God
God wouldn't have given us this baby
If it wasn't
Right

growing

Nestled in
Squirrelled away
Our little secret
Lines getting stronger
You must be growing
You must be making your bed
Revelling in our delight

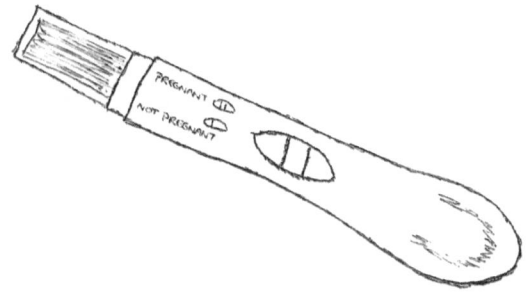

OK

The summer holidays are roaring away
The lizzies are busy
And I'm rushing around
Going from stone to stone
Wood to wood
Splash to splash
Full of the joys of summer
Knowing I'm out and about with
All the babies
Three full of life and one busy growing inside
Knowing that this time next summer
There'll be four outside
And I'll push a pram across the ruined castle grass
Across the sandy shores
Across the twig covered ground
Feeling the utter contentment of knowing that
All is as it should be
So busy those lizzies
They can withstand anything
The summer throws at them
And the fizz fizz of the only drink
You can stomach
Will stop you from drowning
Will banish fear away
We'll have an early scan
We'll know that everything is gonna be
OK

techno beat

Do I get to do this again?
An ultrasound with a techno beat
Everything looks great
So I get to do this again?
Can I be this lucky?
To bring a fourth child home
Could I be this lucky?
Could I?
Squidgy-looking little baby
Wriggling in black and white
Nine weeks young on screen
Heartbeat tapping around the room
Am I pushing my luck?
The echoes of life's beat shake the world
Absorbing everything in its path
I get to do this again.

sing with the birds

There's some sort of magic
Growing
Inside
A special magic
Which everyone tries to hide
Until it's okay
Until it's safe
Until nothing bad can happen
Now everything's going to be okay
We'll shout it from the rooftops
Teach the birds a new song
Because the scans gave their stamp of approval
I mean what could possibly
Go wrong

autumn dreams

Life in the pumpkin patch
In the juicy delight of the
Cinnamon smelling beauty of October
The type of bewitching glory
Heart soaring photography
Instagram uploading
Fever

Where I drive, too early
In a car which was doomed
From the start
Through lanes which make me
Hold my breath
To walk through fields
Of autumn dreams

Pushing a silver wheelbarrow
Filled with pumpkins
Three for them
And one mini one for you
Next year, you'll be able
To hold yours too

it'll be perfect

The flash flash
Of Christmas photography in October
Trying to get three children
To sit and smile
By a fake snow glistened false fireplace
Gosh, next year, there'll be four and
It'll be perfect, in all its chaos

Supermarket trip
On the way back from a scan
Bit of a rush, but let's have a look
A Peter Rabbit outfit
Cotton wool bunny tail, scan print clutching
Evoking my childhood and yours
Gosh, he looks perfect, don't you think?

Let's um and ah
Over his name for a while
Sip away at the dusty days
Feel at ease, feel the nerves
Let's ask the kids what they think
Don't call him that, he sounds like a naughty boy
Little Deer is perfect, all agreed

appearing cracks

Oh I can't see the heart properly
Oh I think you'll have to come back
Oh I think I'll have to refer you
Oh I think you'll have to see a specialist
Oh I think I'm fed up of driving to these appointments
Oh I think you'll need a more in-depth check
Oh I think you need an MRI
Oh I think I'll tell them I'm fed up
Oh I think the significance is unknown
Oh I think it'll all be okay
Oh I think this might all be a fuss over nothing
Oh I think you might want to consider an amniocentesis
Oh I think that's all we've got left to try
Oh I think it'll all be okay
Oh I think it's not good news I'm afraid

lost clock

There you are
My littlest one
Dressed as Harry Potter
On the day we found out
On the day two lines peeked into view
On the day you graduated
From littlest one
To big sister

On a day that felt warm inside
Like coming in out of the cold
And huddling down
Because everything was gonna be
Alright now
In the summer sun
With no fear of burning, just a glorious glow
The lockdowns and daily counts
Were nearing their end
And our baby would be something good
Out of a rancid time

Here you are, my middle one
Soon to lose that title
I know how joyous you'll feel
To have a little brother
It's sixteen weeks
And you're skitteringly perfect
In your excitement
Head resting on my stomach
Safe in the hearth, safe in the home

The summer is drawing to its close
With abandon welcome
Smiling but pushing us out the door
It's the next season's job
To slowly pull the rug
And we will bounce around
Hearing I'm sure it'll be fine
While the crunch crunch
Of the fallen leaves
Sound tuneless
And the sprinkle covered cake
Of another celebration
Tastes not quite right

There you are
The oldest one
Golden in your smile
Sensing things aren't okay
Why do they keep going off
For a whole day
Just wanting the baby born
So that life can resume
On the cusp of knowing
That life can end too soon

Winter ushers in its chaos
With its change of home
With its barren lands
With tests and tiredness
And difficulty functioning
With a grasping hope
Slippery like ice
But still believing that he'll be okay
That we'll all be okay
Ignoring the ticking
From a clock
We can't find

with the faeries

There he was flying through the sky
Come and join me, he said from up high
I can't, I can't, I'm shackled to the earth
I'm heavily with child and I'm due to give birth
Just come with me now, you know it's your fate
Jump up in the air and fly before it's too late

silence the bell

I sit by myself
On New Year's Eve
Waiting for midnight to ring in
But wanting it not to
Every ring of that stupid bell
In the tower bearing my own name
Which I once ran past in defiance
Of infertility and negativity
Trying to be positive about life
Going head first into 26.2 miles
But now
Each wrangling pang of that bell
Shuddering my heart
In fear
I don't want to see what the new year will bring
I don't want to live in the month of January
I need to stay trapped
In the MRI machine of
December
Where I grit my teeth and do it
In the hopes of good news

But now the new year is laying in front of me
And I can feel it internally
There will be no celebration
There will be no fresh page of
A notebook waiting patiently
For bright ideas and dreams
Just the never-ending sadness
Of how life
Can break your heart
And leave you to mourn
In the winter's depths
With no promise of spring's new life
For comfort
Just a clanging bell
For the worst countdown imaginable

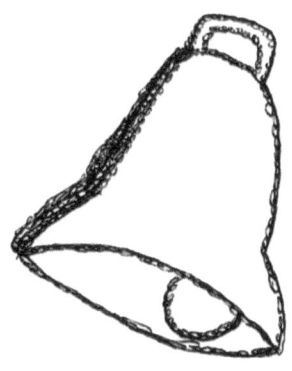

unknown number

I'm waiting all day
For the phone to ring
To give me the good news
All clear
13, 18, 21
Those numbers won't need to mean anything
To us
Because you'll be okay
The doctor told us
I don't expect it to be any of those

I'm sitting on my sofa
Waiting
No number. Withheld
It's the doctor
He's about to say it
The initial results were all clear
He's pausing
But he's going to say it

But he doesn't
He doesn't say it
It's not good news
I'm afraid
The amnio is positive
For trisomy 18
Edwards' Syndrome
The numbers fly through my mind
13, 18, 21
18 was bad
18 meant devastation
He's not going to survive, he said
We need you to come in to discuss options

I can't, I said
My baby is going to die
He's 33 weeks
I can't
Discuss options
You see
My whole world just crashed around me
Into the smallest pieces
I'll never find all these shards
They'll never fit back together
I have to go, I said
I'll call you back
I said

edwards' syndrome

Falling into a
necessary
sleep

Waking with a
hit
of words

The two words
pop
into my mind

All night
waking
mind and body

The two words
that will
take you

from me

bursting

Thirteen days
Where we sat
Floating in floods of big fat tears
Thirteen days of hellish limbo
Where we knew this wasn't heading
Anywhere good.
Going about our days as normal but dazed
The school run, barely able to walk along
Womb fit to burst
Driving, listening to nineties songs
The Cranberries' Dreams reverberating
Was it all a dream?
A sick, twisty, kaleidoscopic dream
Where he's born and they say, oh sorry
We were wrong
Or one where he's not even there at all
A beautiful mirage
Of a broken mind
But thirteen days of sickly torture
Starting with a phone call
And ending with a slow drip of water
That would end up drowning us all

in between

Alive in the petulant
Tempestuous sea
Ocean spray, soggy sand
Stuck in between everything
That was when life changed
With the ring ring of an anticipated call
That was the split
Then, now
Locked in the befall
Just a simple ring
Now those sands, they are sinking
Now those waves, they are battering
And life is spinning out of control
There's salty water
Stuck in my mouth
And I can cling on to the buoy
For dear life
Even though I know it won't save
Yours

trembling calm

You're swimming
In litres and litres of fluid
Blissfully unaware
Blissfully beautiful
Not knowing
That your life
Will be so short
That no amount of love will save you
But Mummy will keep you safe
Until I can't anymore
Until my body gives up on us
Until the fluid drip drops away
And you'll have to be born
And I'll hold you through the trembling calm
And I'll tell you you're beautiful
My beautiful boy
And I'll tell you I love you

I'll say
Hello sweetheart
Again and again
And you'll open your eyes
While our faces touch
And I'll worry that my cheek is covering your nose
And I'll keep stroking your face
Until your breaths slow
And your eyes close
And you fade away
So far away
But I'll still
Never want to let you go

just the low

How could January be so cruel
To turn life into a morphing juxtaposition
To tear a baby from the warm embrace of comfort
To take a piece of all of us away
January
The month where hope died
No promise of a fresh start
Just the low.
The low of lives forever changed
The twinkling lights of December lost forever.
The joy of anticipation left on the doorstep
As the new year rang in
The fear climbing the ladder inside me
Afraid of what might be coming

Take all your Januaries and banish them
Because
Death's arrival is imminent
And no words or hopes or dreams
No power on Earth
Can stop it

effervescent hope

I think they're wrong
The words, so raw, impacted with hurt
This effervescent hope
So beautiful in its motives
Lingers in the stuffy air
Of our hospital room
As I lay in wait
With the water's rush
And the positive swabs
As the surgeons prep

The scan showed us
You're engaged
Your heart's still beating
It's time
Unfortunately
But I'm not ready
For this
I thought I had two more weeks
Before I had to face this
This unknown

Those words are still
Hanging in the air
Unmistakable hope
The kind that hurts
The kind that bursts out
In audible sobs
Takes your breath and catches it
But doesn't give it back
I think they're wrong, he said
I hope so, I thought

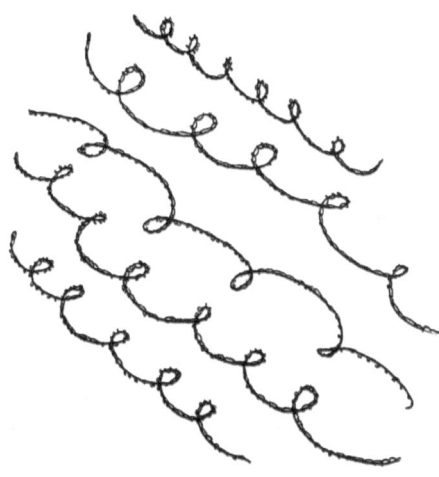

live

The noise of an operating theatre
Is deafening
When breath is held
In anticipation of your exhale

To cry is to breathe
By yourself
The silence, it builds up
The fear screams inside, the outside is dazed

How do these moonlight dreams
Keep floating
In the harsh lights of artificial sun
Where your life has only just begun

The only cry you'll ever make
Brings a small reprieve
After the three thousand years
Of silence

All the life-led thoughts
Followed by death-laced fears
Oh God, please, just please
Let him live

sparks

If stardust should fall
On your head
I would spin around
And laugh
For you are made
Of such sparks

35 weeks
24 hours
53 minutes
With you

harbour nights

When people say your name
In an English accent
It sounds like Ocean
And I felt like I was on a boat
Being pushed through corridors
On a hospital bed
Holding you like any mother would hold
Her newborn
Except you'd died
Hours ago
And I was moving
With the sea
Spilling my guts
Over the side of the boat
Outside the lift doors
Waiting to go to a room
Where the butterflies fly
In the perfect silence
Of the cold cot
And the peaceful flutter
Of wings
Over lapping water

your place

Walking into the hospital
pregnant
And walking out
With empty arms

With pain stealing your place
Pain that rips and tears
At our earth's foundations

That walk away, from you, from that time
Knowing there'll never be a way back.
Just walking, feet stuck muddy and heavy

No car seat gently swinging from
the crook of an arm
Just a quiet trudge to the car

No faffing around to install the seat,
while being as gentle as a tip-toeing fairy
Because that was only present in a future
That's ebbed away as the day diminishes into night

No tender glances, no internal excitement
to take the new baby home
No worrying whether they'll wake for milk
as the car bumps and hums along the road.

Just the shock, just the numbness
Just the loss

Just outfits not needed
Just prams, just cots, just milk
Spilled
Drying up, given away, hidden
Just empty space

Where you should be

Just loss breaking
Just loss taking
Your space

It hurts because we love
They said
Hurts because we love with our whole beings
Flip-sided love

It's love, it's grief, it hurts, it really hurts
And it spins and it twirls, out of control

But when it stops

It's just love

Just love lingering
Just love lasting
Just love filling
Your place

everywhere

Tangled up in the darkest time I've ever known
Is the brightest spark of light
So small, so precious
Yet huge.
Overflowing all the stadiums of the world
Just love, exquisite and patient
Better than the most vibrant dream
More real than the Earth itself
I wanted you to stay
The only thing to eclipse the back-breaking pain
Is love
World-changing love
I would do anything to have you here
Hold you tight to my chest in the utter banal
To push you in a pram, hand grabbing for the rain cover

You're a blessing so vast
A flame so fearless
A life so short
A magic so complete
An impact deeper than the widest of all valleys
Eternity holds us in the love we share
You will light our lives
Baby boy
You are part of the
Stardust that radiates
Everywhere
A light that cuts through
Any darkened sky

parquet flooring

I took a photograph
Of scuffed parquet flooring
Brown, zig zag, old
We were sitting in a room
At the register office
Plucked from the wait
Ushered to a quiet space
Choking in the nippy air
Scraping chairs and heels on wood
Away from the other people
Happy to register their baby's
Birth

I stared down at this parquet flooring
A room used for planning
Weddings
And joyous occasions
Where sparkles light the room
From bright eyes and coy smiles
A makeshift space for two people
In the deepest of shocks
A wait of a thousand moons
A thousand sunrises and sets
Just this zig zag flooring
And spinning thoughts

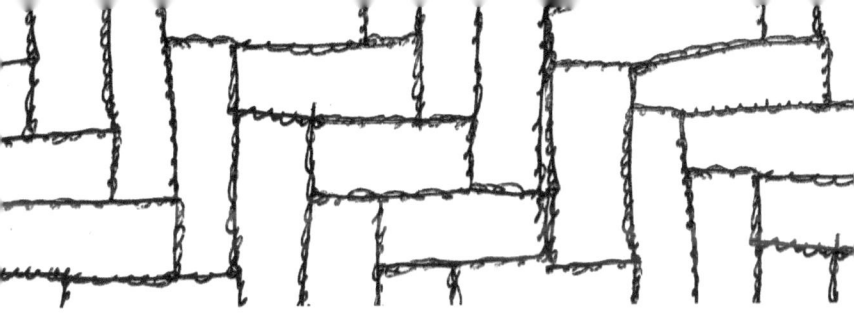

Just about a week
Since he died
Since we had to walk away
From his body
And about ten days until
His funeral
Where we would have to walk away
From his body
Again
We have to register a birth
And a death
Both his
And see it in printed text
Feelings smothered
In black letters
S t a m p i n g
Their finality
A life lived of only
53 minutes

Is this stardust floating through the air
Or just the ashes of those who aren't there
Are the wet patches on the floor
From rain covered shoes
Or tears, rivers of tears
Overflow
I don't know
Would you join me in these
Emotionless motions
With the gracious registrar
Aware that the couple before us
Had their baby with them
Sitting on the floor, no doubt
In its carry car seat
Taking their time
Savouring this significant moment

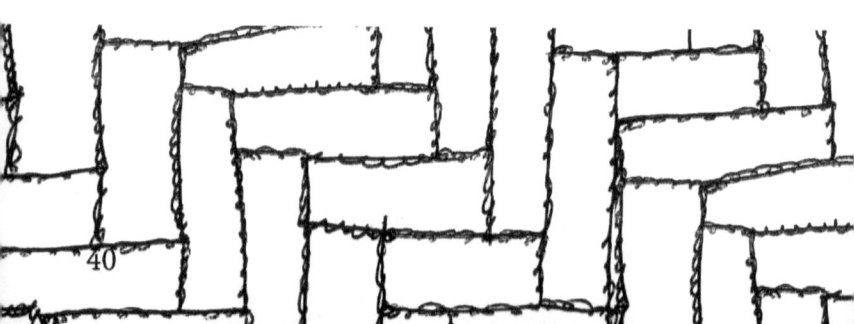

Why would I take a photograph
Of that flooring
In that room
Of that moment
What purpose did early morning
Grief think it would serve
Should I have pointed the lens
Upward
To face the sky instead
To scramble in this intake of breath
To scream
From the bottom of your feet
Out of your mouth and into
The ether
There's no space this
Pain cannot reach

We won't come back
Until the funeral
Over a week later
Just Mummy, Daddy, baby
And the ground
The cold, dark ground
With the freshly dug earth
From which all beauty flows
We will throw a flower each
And they'll perfectly cross
One over the other
White like the cleanest
Snowfall
Green like the richest, buoyant
Life

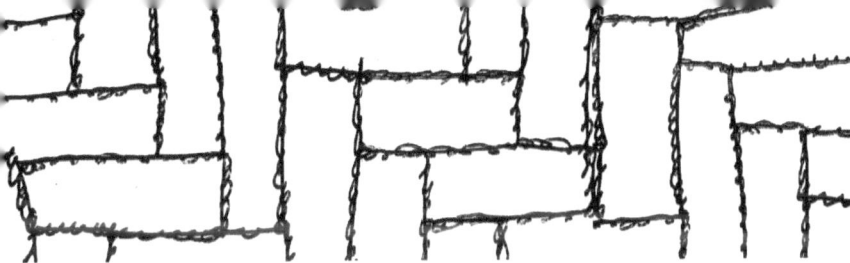

But can we smash it all up
Tear it all into pieces
And start again
Bring it all to a standstill
And restart
Spin the Earth on edge
So the phone rings differently
So the voice says
Good news
It's all clear
It's all okay
I've seen your future and I've
Taken all the pain away
No numbers need to matter here
Because he's okay

And you'll go to the register office
And you'll bring home
One certificate, not two
And there'll be no funeral
No rain soaked earth
Where you'll drive off
Leaving your baby in the ground
Desperate to run back and wrench
The coffin from the soil
You'll just be at home
With him
Being normal
In the rays of starlight
That new humans bring
To the world

And the only brokenness you'll feel
Will be lack of sleep
Not like there's a piece torn
Away from your core
Where you'll replay watching
Him die
In your mind
During casual conversations
And while watching TV
And you'll cry those tears
That pull hurt through your whole
Body
Those Earth shattering tears
The ones that you weep
With a guttural pain
Begging time to rewrite
For phones to ring differently
And for forces more powerful
To intervene

dust-covered

Too little time in this world
Too much heartbreak left behind
A cot. A pram. Clothes.
Never slept in. Never sat in. Never worn.
I talk to you all the time
Silence responds
I write letters to you
But I have no address to post them
And the book of stamps is dust-covered
My arms remain empty
And they ache
For you

love is circular

53 minutes
53 years wouldn't be enough with you
53 decades would feel like short change
Time like a grain of sand
Love like a galaxy of stars
Grief breathed in like oxygen

★
Do you look
down
When I look
UP
★

♥

Do you send
your love
to us
in
the whispers
of the wind

♥

old earth

The rain falls down on the old stone
And new earth
The old earth has gone
I don't recognise this new one
One where my baby has Edwards' Syndrome
That syndrome that I've only just heard of
That happens to other people's babies
So tragic
So terrible
But to other people
Not me
Not my baby
Gosh isn't that awful
I'll say, reading someone else's story
Where their baby died
Because of extra chromosomes

But not me
Not my baby
Not on old earth
This new earth is wrong
I'll sing along as hard and loud as I can
To drown out the old stone
And new earth
Where it's me
Where it's mine
Where my baby has Edwards' Syndrome
Where my baby dies
Where my baby died
In front of my eyes
As I longed for the old earth

just

It's just

It's just everything's sad
It's just I don't know
It's just everything hurts
It's just I'm falling apart
It's just we didn't know
It's just it physically hurts
It's just a random chromosomal error
It's just that he won't survive
It's just he can't breathe well
It's just your water's broken
It's just early labour
It's just an amniocentesis
It's just the end of my world
It's just

My baby died

ablaze

By a small light
The room is lit
By a small life
Love is set
For eternity
You took part of me with you
I'll never be as I was before
I don't want to be
I want to huddle by a small light
And set my world ablaze
While death lingers, darkening and choking
Reaching for a hand that's not there
Wanting a cuddle that's just a memory
Hearing a cry that's only present in a diminishing echo
Less than an hour
With eternal impact
And love that bursts from my chest
In painful gasps
And an ache
A desperate ache
To be with you

your january skin

January is the cruellest month
Cruel in its icy relentlessness
Wretched in its closed box of miracles
There's no key to unlock this box
It all happened so quickly
It all happened before I could even sit down
I wanted to keep your little body
Hold you close
Feel your January skin, cold against my face

I want to replay your hour of life over and over
Like your favourite film you watch because you know
How it ends
Because the love I feel for you is bigger
than I ever dared dream
It shocks me with its abundance
And your perfect little face will light my dreams forever more
No dream would be right without your presence

I held you so, so close
Despite my shaking, a supernatural calm I tapped into,
a calm for you
I didn't want your life to be lived
In the wailing of my pain
Moments so precious I hope I never lose them
I pray to God I'll never lose them
I'll never know how it feels to not look death in the face
And watch it leave with someone I love
I won't forget you
I want to look around and see you wherever I gaze

Though I watched death take you
I feel God received you
Your life will do more good
Than we could ever know
My baby you'll always, always be
In the operating theatre, with my abdomen cut open
I will always live

seeping through

Life in this liminal space
What dawn breaks over the tump
Of rock and soil
And grass torched by the rays
The return route is blocked
By impossibility
A thick glass wall
Both impenetrable, immovable
And blurred
Glasses dirtied by smudgy fingers
And hands tapping out words and words
Indulgent in their claptrap
Embarrassed by other people's potential opinion
In this liminal lunacy
Where moving forward
Means leaving you behind
So why can't I take you with me
For fear of judgement
And isn't it time you got over this?
Would you like to get over death?
Use a brush to sweep it away
But it leaves dusty crumbs all over the floor
As the sweeping can't contain it all
The bits seep through the bristles
So where are we?

old stone

Hold my hand as we walk
Through the cemetery. On a beautiful day like this
The birds have built their nests in the bare trees
They sing their song
It hums through the wind
Making the daffodils swish
And the leaves wave
The sun shines down on the old stone
And the new earth
Marking where you lay
Marking where they all lay
He walks with me
On a beautiful day like this

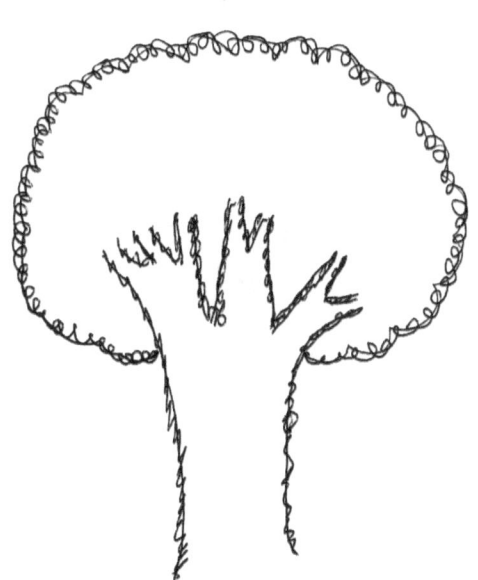

lost but found

I'll find you in the raindrops
In the movement of the treetops
In the warmth that the sunlight leaves on my skin
In the aching feeling ruminating within
In the nip of the frosty air
In the wind rifling through my hair
In the wave of the sea
In the feeling there's a part missing from me
In the snow that drifts slowly from above
In the knowledge that there's no ending to our love

scribbles

Write a poem about the pain you're feeling
It won't help it go away
It won't help you come back
It won't help time be rewritten
Or the stars realign
So that your cells shake off the extra chromosomes
So that my body grows you stronger
So that when you're born there's an almighty cry
From both of us
Not silence revived by oxygen
Not a weak cry and silent tears
But a strong noise signalling the promise of a life
Where my heart is whole
And you are here
Not in limited photographs
Or memories I'm clinging to like the string of a balloon
The only way my pain can truly heal
Is if time gets rewritten
The clock tick tocks backwards
To conception
To the cells
Where I ask them not to include the extra chromosomes
So that you don't have to die
And I could live
Without pain

useless letter formation

Words I feel right now
Sad, but who doesn't feel sad sometimes, eh?
Loving, yes don't we all
Low, these come before the highs; hang on
Calm, after the storm
Blessed, well you have three other kids
Broken, you'll be okay though
Fearful, don't feel that, it won't happen again
Ok, oh that's good
Devastated, it'll get better
Traumatised, this too shall pass
Lost, do some grounding exercises
Found, see I said just pray more
Hopeful, you've got a lot to be happy about
Hopeless, cheer up, it could be worse
Loved, you've still got your family
Pained, take a paracetamol
Alone, you're surrounded by people
Frenzied, you need to calm down now

mother's day

Gratitude and grief
Walk hand in hand
They skip and stumble
Together

life in the long grass

The rough is much stronger
Than the smooth
The days creep along
With a rattlesnake nestled
Waiting
In the long grass
Knowing that everything is so terribly hard
Feeling like an emptiness will always live inside
Always be missing
The rough days in their abundance
Relentless in their rattling
When the smooth seeps
From the corners of the days
The rattle shakes
Scares it away
Life in the long grass
Life in the sway
Life knowing that nothing will ever
Take this pain away

dissipate

Rasping at the door
But I'm not letting you in
With your icy breath
And your frozen fingers
I'm not defrosting my freezer
To get rid of your energy
So take your sneaky Jack Frost nose
And dissipate into the air
Because this is hard enough
Without you
Making me slip over
When I'm trying desperately
To stand

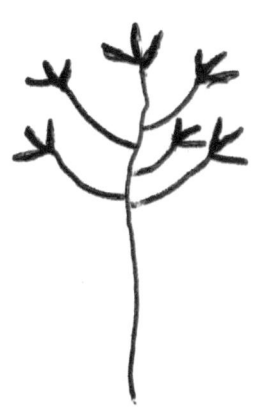

blurred views

When I drive along the road
Music playing of no relevance
I make the words fit
I turn them to you
I see you in my mind
Quiet
Still
My eyes full with tears
Vision blurred
The kind that Specsavers couldn't even help
Blink and keep blinking
You're there in my mind
Looking like my husband
Gosh, doesn't he look like your husband?
Yes
But he's quiet
And still

easter days

Take a family photo
On Easter Sunday
He is risen indeed
Search for chocolate eggs
In a new patch of grass
Where the rain hasn't muddied the path
Pink, yellow and blue foil-covered delights
Bowls overflowing with giggles
Watch Dawn French dress as the Easter bunny
Because you always do
Subduing the ravaging fires of grief
Fill your tummy with the feast
But take a photo
All together, your family
Hear a sermon about the resurrection
Read a book about the Easter bunny
We can't dig you out of the ground
With the saddest tinge of darkened sky
Lean into the softly simmering joy
With five sitting together
Squished on a two-seater sofa
And one photo in a frame clutched
Tightly between the hands
Of your eldest, with unabashed grin
To make six
Acknowledging the missing piece

wallow

There's beauty in the world
But I don't want to see it
There's kindness
But I don't want to feel it
Because everything is wrong
Everything is sinister
Everyone's got an ulterior motive
And I don't want to see any good anymore
Because you were good
So good
And yet you couldn't stay
So I don't want to see beautiful
Hear stories of miracles
Or other people's joy
Because you're gone
And the light has gone away from life
The beauty is barren
And the kindness is putrid
And my weary heart is broken
And I will never see the good in
Anyone
Or anything
Again

i see you

I was thinking
My love
How you are here
Even though you're not
How you not only live on
In my heart
But all around us
Like unquestionable magic
Like the snap of frosty breeze
Like the dew on a grass blade
Unnoticed often
But always there

robin

Little robin on my fence post
Can you stay awhile
Can I quench your thirst
With a saucer of water
Or throw some seeds in the air
To satisfy your hunger
I wanted you to come
Here
Today
You've never been here before
Or since
But fleetingly you showed up
And I saw you
Transiently
Red-breasted and eager
Heavy with symbolism
Lighter than your own feathers
Blood red from the cross

On a day to review
To talk
To understand
To float around in a strange existence
Where apparently my child
Died
And today we relive it
In the hopes of the blame
Sifting off our bodies
As the words tumble around the room
Guided by professionals
Later that day
In their special releasing way
Before flying off
Into the air
With you
To soar, to breathe through
Wings at one with all the things
We cannot see

tidal wave

A memory just flooded back
Like a wave in my mind
Not seeping under a doorframe
But crashing into the room
Leaving watermarks everywhere

Oh, your heart is racing
she said
As I lay there, waiting
Yes, well I'm frightened
My mind thought
I think we are both going to die here
In this operating theatre
I think my placenta will tear away
And I'll bleed to death
My heart is racing
Because I know he is going to die
And I think I might too

first times

The first time I took you to Aberystwyth
It was only in my mind
The first time you graced the beach
It was only in the letters of your name
The first time you played in the castle playground
It was only in my imagination
The first time you felt the spray of the choppy sea waves
It was only in your name stamped onto my jewellery
The first time you walked the town streets
It was only in my heart
The first time you went to the sweet shop
It was only in my thoughts
And my desire to buy a little windmill
to place at your grave

your name in the sand

I'm on the sand
With your daddy, your sisters
And your brother
I write your name in the sand
Because I want you to be with us
Because I can
Each letter etched into the slightly wet sand
Each letter leaving a little moment
A little imprint
A little reminder to the world
That you were here
You lived
You deserve to be remembered
And all the beaches, all the seas
Should know your name
And the water should carry your name
Everywhere
Until there's not a sea creature that has not heard
The whisper of your name carried through the oceans
Because you were here
And you matter

Every cloud will send down your name
On every raindrop
And splash it everywhere
So that every human on Earth will be touched
By your memory
And every puddle will tell your story
Of how you and your short life
Could create so much love
That even the waves cannot comprehend it
As they slither
And sometimes crash
Over the etched letters
Of your name in the sand
And the love you brought to the world

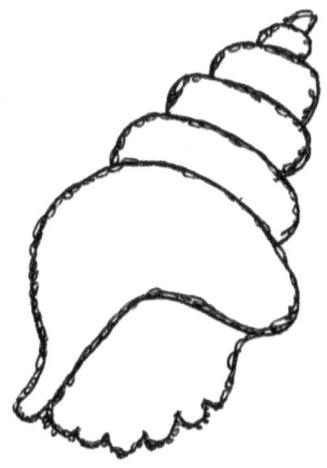

did you?

Did you feel me, Mum?
As I clung to your arms
As you pulled the weeds up
Around my grave

Did you hear me, Mum?
As the wind whispered
I love you
In the wisps of the breeze

Did you see me, Mum?
As the light and rain made a rainbow
As the sun set
Bleeding colours across the sky

Grief

I don't know what grief is
I only Live it

who's there?

There you are
Knocking at my door
Every day
Trying to steal my peace
You're not a person
You're a thief
Of time
Of life

There you are
Knocking at my inner door
Trying to break me from the inside
Out
You're the feeling that tries to squeeze in the door
When grief has entered the room
Trying to make it about you
About disaster
About gloom
About how life will never ever be any good
Ever again
How you'll never feel anything other than fear
Ever again

There you are,
The repetition
That burns into my mind
Look for danger
What you seek
You'll find
Because you've seen that
Sometimes
The worst case
Actually happens
And now you're there
Knocking
Knocking
Knocking
At my door

call back later

Sometimes
I feel alone
In my grief
Like no one understands
No one gets it
And they're all so busy
Sorry I didn't text
It's been hectic
Yeah, it's been hectic here too
Living the worst year of my life
Trying to be a mum to four
Three living
One dead
Seeing other babies
And knowing he's dead
Knowing he'll never do
Or see
Or be
Like those other babies

And I'll never be able to feel whole
Or feel ok
Again
So I'm alone
In how I feel
Sympathy slips away
Or so it seems
Because everyone's too busy
To remember
But like a primal rumbling
Like a fixed mark on the horizon
I won't ever
Forget

missing

I don't know what you're meant to say
You're a father of four
But only three are alive
I don't know how these special days
Are meant to go
When there's always a missing person
In any party
At any meal
During any lazy day
A hole that gapes with a sadness that won't quit
Father's Day comes around
And I sign his name on your card
Because he never will
But I can
And I will
Because you're a father of four

Even if one is not calling your name
And asking for a drink
And moaning
Because they want the TV on
Or crying
Because their sibling took their toy
Even if that one can only be felt
in the whisper of the breath of the wind
Or the beat of a robin's wings
through the invisible air
Or in the shadow of suggestion
in a family photo
Where we see him but no one else does
These special days keep hitting that bit harder
Because we know
He's missing
And the ache is relentless within our hearts

unconditional

Your existence alone
Guaranteed you'd be loved
Forever
You didn't need to do a single thing
To earn love
To be wanted
You were just loved
For being there
And you'll always be loved
Without doing anything
Without saying anything
Without accomplishing anything
For just being you
For just existing
And I will sit here and hold
Your teddy bear
Under my chin
Until my tears flow enough
To water the world's trees
Evergreen
And evermore

Just thinking about
The love
I have for you

the boy who lived

Can I freeze time?
Right when you were alive
When you were breathing
When your eyes we're looking at me
And let me realise the significance of the moment
Let me know that this was the only time you'd ever do this
Hammer it home to me. This moment will never come again
Help me take it all in just that bit more
Let me ask someone to take more photographs
Let me ask them to take different photographs
Just freeze the bloody time please
Let the beep beep of the machines replace the ticking
Let me live in this moment
Where you're alive
And I realise that you're really looking at me
And I realise that you never will again
And we can look at each other more
And I can tell you I love you more
In this moment
Where no one is dead
And there's a flicker of hope
That you might be the boy who lived
Not just for 53 minutes
But for a lifetime
Where you grow old
And watch me die instead

floating words

The trees are growing fat
In the summer days
The sky is slashed blue and pink
In the summer sunsets
In the evening before the day slips into night
Where the quiet becomes louder
And the questions become deeper
And the tearing from the inside rips a bit wider
Like a drawl that keeps going
Uncomfortably long
The summer sunset has gone grey
The quiet is intrusive
A tyre scraping the road is pricking my senses
And the lack of light is breaking down
This is where the fairies fly
And the questions become unanswerable
But they clatter down all around
Like the smash of hail stones
As the water rises and threatens to overflow
But the questions don't wash away
They bounce on the top
Buoyant in their defiance

awkward days

Please don't ask me how I am
Unless you want the real answer
I'll say I'm okay
Because I know you don't want to really know
Because if I tell the truth
It'll be awkward
And it's awkward enough already
It's searing already
I feel how I'm an awkward moment in your day
Best avoided
God forbid you have an awkward moment
in an otherwise fine day
So don't ask me how I am
Unless you're ready to
Be awkward
With me

twirling around

Do you want to take my hand?
And we can dance this awkward dance
Together

It's left side up and right side down here
The place where love and grief
Flow

safe in the tipping down

Someone's gotta like the rain
Someone's gotta love the rain
Someone's spirits have to lift as the clouds crowd
And the drizzle slithers down through the grey sky
Seeing the beauty in the puddle shadows
Feeling an instant calm at the sound of the drops hitting the house, the ground, the car
Someone's gotta feel like everything is being washed clean
Smells like rain out there
Pour it down over my head
I want to hear the violent drumming
Delighted in the raindrops clinging to window panes
Comfortable in the melancholy
Don't call it off for rain
We're safe in the tipping down
Someone's gotta love the rain tapping against their window
Someone's gotta love it pissing down

take me way back

Driving six counties away
Back and forth
Getting annoyed at the monotony
All a bit excessive, this?
When they don't even think there's anything wrong
With him
Sitting and waiting
Hours and hours
Covid banishing the dads to the outdoors
While the women sit
Stuffy plastic seats along a corridor
Just waiting and waiting
All a bit excessive really
Do we really need to drive this far?
Takes all day
You know
So much driving
So much waiting
And they still say they don't know
But he's going to be fine anyway

I never thought I would say
I never thought I would miss
Those drives
Those waits
Those seats
I never thought I would wish
To make those drives again
To endure those waits again
To feel impatient
To tell them we have to leave
We cannot wait any longer
And do we even really need to be here?

But he was alive
And his life was assumed
His future was anticipated
Because he was going to be okay
He might need some help
But he would be okay
On those drives
On those seats
He was alive
It was just inconvenient
It wasn't serious
He was going to live
And they were being OTT

So please, God
Take me back
Take me way back please
To those drives along the M4
To those frustrating traffic jams
Those waits on those hard seats
Those awkward moments
Trying to produce a urine sample
with an unlocked door
To impatience
To unabashed hope
To sheer belief
That he would live
That a life would lay itself before him
And to knowing that everything would be okay
On those drives
In those seats
Six counties away

waiting for the phone to ring again

When things go wrong
Then tend to go very wrong
He said to me
On the phone
As I sat in my car
In the school car park
No longer nervous but
Jaded in the afternoon rush

Months before the phone
Had rung again
He was already dead
Yet it continued its trill
More results
More stuff amiss
Worry to gnaw around inside
To eat away at the remaining shreds

He had an extra copy of 18
That, we knew
But 3 and 21 also decided to swap
To rearrange
To break off
To make new
Pity though, those chromosomes
Were mistaken
Their route erroneous

Unbalanced translocation
Trisomy
Things I'd never heard before
It happened to you
But now we might be balanced
We might have sent the translocation
Downstream
Where it made your life even less likely
Yet I carried you for 35 weeks

So we wait in a more minor limbo
To see if it's me, to see if it's him
I mean surely he couldn't have been this
Unlucky
Picking at some old wallpaper
Trying to expose the truth
It must be us
I feel genetically absurd

And then it comes
The result
Over the phone, once more
In a static caravan, where I scramble
For signal
Where I pause for breath
And then it turns out
Mummy and Daddy are both normal

And despite his misguided chromosomes
To me, he was never
Wrong

two steps

I'll run and run
Until my lungs hurt
I'll dance and dance
Until my feet bleed
I'll sing and sing
Until my heart's out

And I'll still be
Two steps behind you
At all times

unpurchased

Little blue triceratops
I reached for it for you
But couldn't buy it
I thought about you all the way round
Through the grey drizzle
Through the shrieks and giggles
Of the rosy-cheeked children
Who moaned about being cold
Through the sandwiches
Being watched closely by fat seagulls
But I couldn't buy you the triceratops
Because you weren't there
And the little robin that caught my attention
wouldn't have appreciated it
Little blue triceratops
I wish I'd bought you

bubbles

Bubbles pop across the blue sky
These bubbles we've released for you
Dear babies
It was meant to tip down
But it's dry and blue
The only thing that's missing is you
We've lit a candle
We've scattered petals
We've listened and spoken
And cried
We've prayed to God or sat in silence
And these bubbles continue to fly
As they bounce in the wind
Their direction unknown
Till all of a sudden they're gone
And we cannot follow
We can only watch the rainbow-coated bubbles
Perfect in the sunlight
Perfect in splendour
Until they're out of our reach
And visible only in our memories

just so loved

How have these months gone by
Since I first saw your face
In front of me
Not on a screen
Since I first held your hand
And touched your skin
Not on a scan print
You should be laughing now
You should be trying to sit up
You should be so curious about what's going on
Around you
Miserable as your gums teethe
Consoled by cuddles and warmth
We should be living our lives with you alive
Not living our lives visiting your grave
You should be with us now
In person
Not in spirit
It's not getting any better now
This time is not healing
No matter how many months wiz by
Our hearts will sing a lament for you
From the tips of our toes to the tops of our voices
And our arms will ache to hold you
Because it'll never be okay
It'll never be alright
You'll always be loved
And ever so missed

hand in hand

Some days it's unbearable
Some days it's so painful my breath catches in my chest
Some days I replay watching you die
Over and over
While I get on with
Life

weep with the willow

I'm sitting on a bench
At the start of summer
As the sky is bright blue
And the clouds fluffy white
The threat of sunburn lurks
But my feet don't touch the ground
The bench is high and my legs are short
So I swing my legs
And watch your brother and sisters play
Climbing and laughing and shouting and fighting
And I sit on the edge of tears
All day every day
Because this isn't how it should be
Where there's three there should be four
And where there's space

It should be filled
And you should be here crying because you're
Hungry or tired or teething
Or just want to be held
I want to be held
I want to cry
I want to cry in the midday sun
I want the wind to carry this devastation
Through all the leaves of every tree
So every green growth knows
That you should be here
I want the sun to understand this deep longing
I want the shade of the willow tree
To weep with me

ever lit

What's this flood of light
Another social media post
Light a candle tonight
Let the flame brush the window pane
Let it burn through the emptiness
But it's not for them
It's for the world that forgets
It's to remember the sparks
They're already aware
They live in aware
It's for the moved on, the banished out of mind
Become discontented
Become smouldering, flickering flame
To switch on a lamp to illuminate the echoes
By all this sharing
By all this remembering
Spread awareness, thick like buttered toast
On a frosty morning
To remember them
To say I know you lived
All the ever lit candles
Overcoming the darkness
Because they know
Because they remember
But the ever-spinning everyday humdrum,
The shake it off and walk away, doesn't

arise

We are not meant to survive
A loss like this
We are meant to
Die with you
And be reborn from the ashes
Each speck seeking the other
Confused and in pain
Until a shadow of a person
Emerges
Functioning
Looks normal from the outside
But forever missing a part
Forever cracked
The specks unsealed in their smouldering form
A different person lives
The old one died
With you

on the cusp

I almost did it
I almost had the dream
Four kids
Two girls
Two boys
My idea of
Perfect
After all those years
Of infertility
Of IVF
Of months of nothing
Of early miscarriage
Of failed treatment
Of keeping going
Of giving up
The four of you turned up on your own terms
At your own time

But the dream slipped away
The dream died
I have three kids
And one grave
One child who'll never grow up
One whose life was complete within an hour
One who I miss with a physical pain
In my chest
I am lucky
I have two girls
One boy
Alive
But it'll never be right
Like a missing table leg
We will never feel complete
We'll always be in danger of toppling
Dreaming of the 53 minutes
Where I had you all

revel in the grey days

The sun's out
People are happy
Smiling, drinking,
Not a care in the world.
No interest in sun cream
I'm gonna get a tan
I'm gonna burn
Everything seems better when it's sunny
Doesn't it?
Everything looks better with
A backdrop of blue blue sky
Don't you think?
So why do I feel like
I'm a square peg
Sitting here waiting for winter
To start

When everyone will be cold
And grey
Revel in the grey days
And not being full of the joys of summer
Will be okay
And I won't have to pretend
That I'm okay
I can just be
In the cloudy days
In the rainy skies
In the lows, in the downtime
In the bare tree time
In the petal-less green shoots
Waiting below ground

oh

Could you get off your phone please?
Oh sorry I was just proofreading a book of poetry
Could you get off your phone please?
Oh sorry I was just looking at photos
of my baby that passed away
Could you get off your phone please?
Oh sorry I was just scrolling and scrolling
to distract my damaged mind
Could you get off your phone please?
Oh sorry it's just I feel so alone
Could you get off your phone please?

Oh. Sorry.

flooding

Too much water
Drowning your roots
Your leaves are turning yellow
Falling off your branches
It's my fault
I'm giving you too much
When I should stand by and
Let you go
Leave you parched
Watch your leaves
Fall to the ground
Leaving room for
New growth
It's just
I planted you
In memory
And I'll never let go

oh my gosh

Gosh what a lot of sharing
These days
How terrible
How sad
Gosh I'm so sorry
It's tragic
I can't even choke out the words I'm sorry
Gosh I'm hoping to say nothing
Pretend this never happened
I don't know how you cope
Gosh you're so strong
But I think it's just for attention
They need to get over it now
Move on

Gosh this is inconvenient
How uncomfortable
How difficult
They're mentioning their baby again
The one that died
Gosh I don't need that today
I don't need to hear about that any day
So often
Gosh same photos
Same old sentiment

Gosh it's for them
For babies, the children
For memory
For honour
Visible absences
Visible heartbreak
Gosh they should be here
Skipping along in the world
But they aren't
Gosh, they can't make new memories
Share new stories
Take anymore photos
Gosh this is all they've got

Gosh it's not for attention
It's not for the poor me
They don't want the world to forget
Their child has gone
Why should their memory be?
Gosh don't close them away
Don't let heart and soul remain
In a memory box
Gosh they lived
Beautiful, tragic, loved
Missed deeper than the fullest ocean

Gosh but I'm uncomfortable
See that's okay
Discomfort can course through you
Breathe through it
Exhale away
Gosh sometimes life really is unfair
Breathe deep and let the bereaved just try
To keep their loved one
With them

phantom

Why do I feel like I can feel you
Moving
When I know you're not there
A sharp kick
Which is only my imagination
Why does my mind decide to have moments
Where it still thinks I'm pregnant
And it's all just been some horrible dream
But it's not
It's my life
And it's your life
And your death
And learning to live
Without you

Getting dirt smeared hands
In the desperate desire to watch something
Grow
Looking for stars
To illuminate this
Black hole
Waiting for rain
To fill the world
With water drops
Because the drip drop
Feels like your magic
Sent down
Like a feather from a bird
Drifting down
Trying to find ways of
Seeing you

We won't be going back
We can only find you now
Where we look
Where my mind tricks with kicks
Where my mind tries to pretend
None of this is real
Waiting for rain to wash
My hands
Where the soil stains
And I keep to myself
The make believe tricks
And the sinking pressure
Of a life snatched away
And a life complete
In 3180 seconds

in dreams, in waking life

I like to think I see you
Every night when I sleep
When I close my eyes
And my thoughts mingle with
My fresh dreams
I like to think we are together
Just together
Soaking up all the time
We are denied
In waking life
In the swirling stars
And the bright rays
Of all the magical darkened light of
The sleeping hours
Hold us

Before the night is finished
And the light floods the earth
And I don't remember
Any of it
Just a feeling
A glorious echo

not sure

I am not sure
How I manage
My days

I am not sure
How I don't
Lose it more

I am not sure
How I listen
To other people's crap

I am not sure
How I keep going forward
When all I want to do is

Go back in time
And freeze it
And live there

In the ice cubes
Wretched in their reluctance to thaw

(not) sharing is (un) caring

Trying not to breathe into the broken
Breathing it in on a count of four, out in six
Shallow breaths and eyes at the sides
I've got two girls
And two boys
She said
Yes, me too
I think
But they're not all here
And I omit my youngest
And I explain my youngest
When asked how many children I have
Because I am not feeling strong today
Because I want to remind the world that he existed
But because I don't know what to say
Without giving the game away
There is no game, there just is truth
Without breathing in the brokenness
With swallowing the brokenness whole
Without letting my guard down

But I'm guardless in your wake
I don't want my voice to choke
Or a tear to fall
Not here
Not now
I let the tears fall
Here
Now
I hold the tears in
Here
Now

So I don't say him
So I tell everything about him
With my shallow breaths
And my eyes dancing around the peripheries
And my eyes looking straight at theirs
Saving the asker from awkwardness
Paying awkwardness into the room
Telling all
Saying nothing
And not relinquishing the small amount of control
I have
Relinquishing every morsel of control
I have

i'm alright

Drowning in the shallow seas
The rock pools and their relentless lapping
Sharp shells and the jellyfish sting
The sand without its paper
Slowly smoothing the edges
While I dance in a life of pretend
Where exhausted white clouds
Are too tired to rain
And grey seas can't be bothered to crash
With the blue sea busy
Looking like it's all okay
But it's all broken
Shells in shards
Seaweed tangled everywhere
Lost in the lazy lighthouse
With a padlock for a sudden stop
But it looks okay
So it must be

Fine

precise magic

Vulnerability is strength
Is it though? The petrol station is closed
I hear this phrase bandied around town
Like it means something
I can't fill up
I've left my profoundness at the wrong junction
Sharing is caring, can you spare a litre?
Who is it caring for?
Is it for me or you, this bus won't wait forever
But are we strong in our weakness
Will the train stop at the next station?
Will a little green shoot
Grow into an almighty green tree?
Steady and powerful in its grounding
Releasing steam from the old train
Sharing the benefits of its knowledge around town
Soaking up every drop of rain and sun
Starting engines, pushing forward
And letting go of the precise magic
The broken need
To breathe

what if it slips

I worry about my memories
Some are grey
Some are bright
Some are fraying at the edges
Some have disappeared completely
So what do I do
If my memories of the operating theatre
Start to dim
What do I do
If my recall stops calling
If I can't remember how it felt
To have your face pressed up against mine
If I can't remember looking into your eye
If I can't remember stroking your face
If I can't remember your cry
What do I do
If I can't remember the pain
Of watching them take you away
Of holding your cold and still body
Of kissing your face
Perfect in its immobility

What do I do
If I can't remember you
And the memories drift off
On a summer breeze
Dispersing across the sky
With the spring blossom
How do I keep you here
When you're already gone
How do I live here
With your cells
When you're already gone
If my brain forgets
Will my heart always know
Will your cells keep telling it
That you'll never go

fly with me

If I could travel back in time
Where would I go?
To you, of course
To hold you so close again
To know what I know now
And then I would take you further back in time
With me

To your brother's first day at school
Where he was beautifully scared but brave
To the countless times we sat cuddled
and watched the same old film
God I'd give anything to watch it again

To your sister's first ballet show
Where you'd get to see her outside of my womb
And you'd feel the depths of pride and emotion
God I'd give anything to sit pregnant with you
Watching her take bold strides on a stage in winter

To your sister's delight in the birds and animals
To walking around and pointing at ducks
While she sits in a buggy or totters along
Asking what's that, what's that
As I smile
God I'd give anything to feel that at ease again

Where else would I go
And where else would I take you
To see all this stuff that's lit my world
Or to times of just being, just sitting, just being held?
Oh God I would do anything to just sit and be held
With you

all round

You'll find me in the night sky
The early mornings
when the drip drip drip
is falling into the coffee jug
You'll see me in the baby laughing,
the hug from an old friend,
the bumble bee bumbling
So important, the bumbling
So essential, the love
The roar of the ocean,
the snap of the bone
The tears of the mind,
the heart, the fear
You'll find me in the midday sun,
the evening drizzle
Seeping through every break
in every heart in every soul
The night cream you cried off

The tap dancing raindrops
You'll find me in the darkness,
in the light
Through the trees,
through the brick,
through the reinforced steel
You'll find me flowing through the air
Through every grain of sand
To every peak,
every low,
every rock bottom
Those mountains,
they will move
Those hearts will be whole
In the splash of the words on the paper,
the screen
I am here,
with you

longing to belong

Sometimes there are no words
And I can't explain how I feel
Big bright bloody good news
Leaves me kicked from the outside
The illuminating light show
From the eyes of an utterly happy face
Leaves me feeling like misery is my only home
I don't know if there's any way to feel different
Bushy tailed benevolence
Leaves me lost in the belonging
All I can do
Is wait
For the feeling to free itself
And pass
And hold on to the heatwave heart
Which bursts into flame scorching all the grass
It passes

in the reprieve

I'm waiting for you
The calm that's meant to
Show up
After the storm ends
I'm waiting for you
Fed up of the storm's reprieve
Showing up again and again

Telling me I'm magnificent
But then chipping away
Eroding the glow and blowing me over
I'm waiting for you
The quiet moment where we gather our thoughts

So distant but ever present
Hovering near but kept slightly away
The calm slipping off
But the rage rains down on me
The storm lives on
I'm waiting for you
In the reprieve

cleansing breaths

I woke up to rain
Little puddles had formed
In invisible wells
The raindrops danced on top
A silly distraction
From the ridiculousness of
Being human
From the words that other people
Think you want to hear
Smugness laced with derision
Are you jealous of what I've got?
Aren't I amazing?
No, you're only as amazing as all the other souls
And jealousy is the enemy's weapon
Wielding comparative envy
To make us make us all feel
Not good enough
Depleted

So God bless the rain
God bless the tap tap tap
When it comes to reset the anguish
And to splash in the face of doubt
Let's dance together in the raindrops
In the pitter patter of fallen water
The one place our broken hearts
Feel seen
The one place
We cannot be
Without

a force bigger

In the blast of a falling wave
In the smash of the storm against the window
In the discord of the morning craze
In the dance of the road commute
In the cacophony of unrest

You will be my opulence of calm
You will be my saviour

don't fear the road

I can't jump over it
I can't slink round it
I can't dig a hole and tunnel under
I can't charter a plane to drop me off the other side
I can't swing over
I can't close my eyes and run
The only way is to barge right through
And get caught in the brambles
Get stuck in the mud
And slowly free myself
One footstep at a time
One bramble at a time

build me a house

The jumble of big, big thoughts
Gives a physical rising sensation
That catches in my throat
Into my jaw
Rattles around my teeth
And wants to be released
As a wondrous sob
Eyes keen to get in
On the act
Make water
Threaten to overflow
These big, big
Evoking thoughts
Turn my insides
Upside down
Unrealisable future
Gone
Moments lost forever
Dreams which will only ever be
Imaginings

But tears
Are a constant
Unwilling to dry up
For something has to spill out
Something has to release itself
Or these big, big thoughts
Will build the biggest house
Of the hardest stone
And a moat to surround it
Watered with
The unshed tears

the girl's not okay

Is it alright if
I say no to life today
Sit at home
With the company of the TV glare

    Is it alright if
    I ignore the phone
    The silent message beep beeping
    I'm going to scroll and scroll instead

        Is it alright if
        I don't go for a healing walk
        Ignore the sea breeze
        Breathe the musty air instead

            Is it alright if
            I don't try and make a positive spin today
            I would like to sit with the sadness
            Because this really is a tragedy

moth eaten

How is it possible to tell people
It's okay, it'll be okay
When I no longer know it to be true
It's like saying oh that orange sunrise
Is actually blue
How do I comfort people
When I don't know what will happen next
And I don't feel self-assured to say
I'm sure everything will be alright
Any wishful thinking hangs by a thread
That's half-eaten by big grey moths
And words catch in my throat
So I stumble out, how about we pray instead?

rough seas, calm waters

Remember when you had your first baby?
Induced and cut out of you?
24 hours waiting for drugs
To soften you up
18 hours ending with fruitless pushing
And no drugs left to pursue?
Remember being taken down
Lying flat
Puking your insides out
And trembling in a 'please get this baby out of me' fear?
Remember her almighty cries that
Kept going?
Do you remember being unwell
Wishing for death, for it all to end
Because surely this wasn't it
Surely this wasn't right?
Remember going back to hospital twice?
IV drips and quiet rooms
Where you saw this reality was tainted
By infections intent on slowly taking
Your life

But do you remember at the end of it
A thriving little baby was awaiting you?
A precious miracle you'd waited for for eight years
Do you remember going straight to theatre
Three more times?
Bringing home two more and leaving one there
To go and lie in the earth?
Only experiencing the breath of this world
for less than sixty minutes
While you looked on helplessly calm
A shocked daze which doesn't ever want to end
Do you remember an easier surgery with a weak cry
and a lot of silence?
Do you remember the staff tip-toeing
Knowing death was knocking on the door?
Do you feel that pain in your guts
When you think back?
When all you can do is buy flowers for the grave
When all you can do is search your memories
for a small detail you may have overlooked
Which you can now blow up, examine and
Make luminous in its shadow

Oh, your heart is racing

So how do you feel
When other wombs bloom and rise
Swelling with the joy of new life
What is your first thought?
Gosh I hope the baby is okay
Gosh I hope they both live
If I stumble and trip over the word
Congratulations
It's not because I don't feel it
Celebratory jigs scare me
In case there's nothing left
When the song comes to an end
When a birth announcement hangs in the air
My first question when it lands is
Are they both okay?
The tinge of fear won't ever leave
So when a birth is smooth sailing
Across a manageable sea
Do I want the waves to crash a little
to experience struggle?

No
I just want everyone to be

OK

surrender

I'm sick but not tired
I'm tired but not sick
Of sleeping
But never feeling rested
Of trying so hard to be positive
And just giving in
Of being angry
Of being angry at people
Living their normal lives
Of missing life before
When stuff like this was just a horrible thought
I could shake off
Oh, the shaking
Now it's life
Now it's the every day
Clinging onto me
But not for dear life

shadows

Can I compare you
To a rainy day
A sudden storm
A windy morning

Can I know you
In my own cells
In my own memory
In the rain that's falling

Can I see you
When I see other faces
Clouds filling blue sky
In siblings dawdling

crowded

Inky squid blackness
Sprawled everywhere
Shoppers go wild
It's a bargain so please beware
Let me go
But to somewhere else
Away from people who don't seem
To have a care
Or they've hidden it
Trodden it down
Everything's so bright, so loud
I'm trying to find some words
But I keep finding the air too deep
Get away from the phone ringing
I just need some sleep
In this sinking sandy room
But I don't want to live somewhere
That gets phone calls like that
So can I sleep in the corner
Of my sofa
With the light on
Where I'm lost
In the palm of your hand
In the replaying
The endless replaying

let's go round in circles

The medication I can no longer
Be bothered
To take
Rattles around the kitchen cupboard

The weight I can't
Be bothered
To lose
Acts like a spare tyre
I just don't need

What are you doing for self-care
This week?
I suppose walking on the grass
In bare feet
Doesn't count?

I suppose ordering another takeaway
Is counter-productive?
I suppose pretending everything is
Okay
Is setting myself up
To fall
Down the stairs
With a clump clump clump

So I cannot even have a thought
Without holding back tears
Again
Yet again
Let's go round and round and round
In circles

And I can't enjoy the view
The stupid bloody view
Because what good is a view
When you're dead

And despite all the wishful thinking
The beautiful, bittersweet dreaming
You won't come again
And I can't
Go back

soul crushed

Is there a baby in your tummy, Mummy?
No darling, it's just swollen with nothingness
The product of too many takeaways and other stuff
In an attempt to feel better
Postpartum slump
In a gluttonous haze

It's too quiet when idle
I don't want to do the devil's work
There's too much room for hurt
There's too much time for sadness
So being busy seems a blessing
But is it possible to get through a loss
Without pretending everything's okay?

Without moving you to my peripheral vision
So I can take care of your siblings
So I can not cry all the time
So I can stop replaying bits of your death
Stop feeling the shaking; revelling in the numbing
But it feels like lying
To everyone

Even happy moments turn sad
With barely a second's notice
All the petals blew off without being ready
Because why should we be happy
Without you
Why would we get to live life
When you can't

What lies am I told
About how I need to act
Gosh don't share too much or you'll upset people
Don't be a rain cloud on my day
What lies am I telling
So that I can function
It is possible to be happy, I know
We can feel joy in ways, at times

Summer holidays are blazing
And we're driving along
Slightly burned sticky skin from sun and lotion
All singing along to Harry Styles
But it's not the same, it can't be
As it was, as he says

Because life will always have that edge
Of emptiness
There'll always be a sickened feeling in my stomach
Like a c-section sag
And the world has left him behind
Already
But I can't stop talking
And I can't move forward
Without him

stages of grief

Bursting with red hot anger
Slicing through the dull grey day
I don't want to hear your stories
I wish you would go away

Red hot poker face
Milk white shawl
How can I be productive
When I feel nothing at all

Crystal blue raindrops drip
Watched by grass green eyes
Going through the motions
But everything feels like lies

recharging

Can we lie down
Just to catch our breath
Just to see if there's some quiet left
This supernatural calm
Only goes so far
And the noise is crashing around
Bumping against the walls

Can we lie down
To gather up some energy
I run out
With no notice
My legs feel like they're stuck
With treacle

Can we lie down
Close our eyes
To catch 53 winks
And wake up
On the other side

rebuild

Amazing what can be achieved
By talking
Fascinating what can be
Reconnected, discovered, rerouted
By purging all these words
All these thoughts
Trying to make healthy pathways
Release old moments
Make sense of the unmakesensible
Rebuild the castle
Breeze block by breeze block
Stone by stone
Pebble by pebble
Dust by dust

Hope

I don't know
what hope is
I only
Hold on
To it

not my friend

Juvenile and fanciful
As lingering as it is laughable
With a picture window
Letting in a sight
People would pay good money for

And I let the grass run wild
Let it lick the window ledge
Green scorched
Submissive thoughts
How do we rue the day again

Because I should
Be grateful
I should think it's wonderful
But it all seems
Not quite right

pebble dashed hope

I saw you, God
Preparing my heart
Helping me be ready
For something you can't be ready for
I see you now
When I look back
Joining dots
And weaving threads
With a rough finish
Placing people on my path
Books on my Audible
Videos on my feed
My heart knew
But my brain didn't
Because I will never get over
A loss like this

Starlight meanders
Helps me see
You're not meant to get over
Death
You're meant to sit with it
And make a pot of tea
So can you ruminate with me
Wave to the distance
Try to draw it close
With pebble dashed hope
We're not meant to
Move on
We're meant to
Move with

no thank you

Warm air circulation
Doing nothing to ease the heat
Of the wave
The sea is warm
The sand is hot
Pale skin is reddening
Gosh we should be thankful
Thankful
The word lands with a thump
Breathing in the sea salt air
Where's your attitude of gratitude
Apparently it'll fix the world
It'll rain down blessings
Like salty spray
You just gotta count them
One by one
Until all you are is thankful
And you'll want no more

Good will burst out of bad
You'll see
There's always a reason
But these sandcastles
Aren't strong
The sand is ebbing away
They're drying out too fast
And I can't find the reason
I can't justify this away
Let the waves come
Let the sun dry this up
Sandcastles are crumbling
In a fallen world

unanswerable

Where are we now
When my oldest son's first thought is
Is he well?
When seeing a new baby
He's barely five
I can read his thoughts on his pensive face
Will another baby have to go?

Where are we now
When my youngest girl
Asks to ring her little brother
Where is he
I can't see him
Ring him, Mum
Please
Please ring him
Please ring him
I can't, my darling, he's not here anymore
And I've got no number to call

Where are we now
When my oldest boy asks
Can we go and dig up his grave and
Bring him home?
Cast aside the flowers and rake up
The wretched dirt
With just our hands

No we can't, sweetheart, no we can't

Where are we now
When my eldest girl asks
Why didn't you get straight into the car and bring him home
So we could take a photo together
So we could hold him whole
I was still in surgery, sweet pea, I couldn't

and I can't call, I can't dig, I can't rush home
I can't comfort
Not in the way I would like

I can only say this is
Life
And love
And death

And connection
everlasting

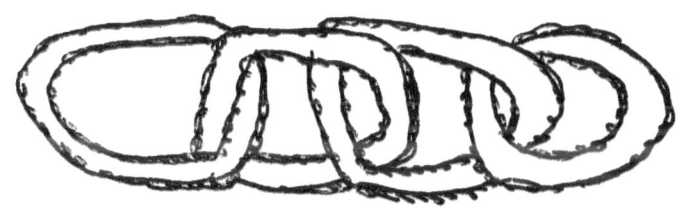

for better or worse

A balm for a lonely soul
A double tap
And an infinite scroll
Making life better for the worse
Instantaneously nauseating
Instantaneous dopamine mine
Is it connection
Is it people, they understand
It's too late to go back
The withdrawn withdrawal
The panic panicking panickers
There's an app for that
You know
If it's possible to feel
So connected
And so alone
It's now
It's this
This life
This screen

plot missing

I'm losing
My plot
If you find
Can you send
Answers
On a postcard
Please

merry-go-round

Can we talk it over
Can we unfuel the fire
Can you help me douse it
Down to manageable ashes
So I can hold it all in two cupped hands
And watch the wind take it all
Away
Those words. Those thoughts
Those washing machine cycle thoughts
Round and round
Sick from the dizziness
My mind, my gut
The ashes
Dispersing through the air
Past the weather-beaten sunflowers
Past the infant silver birch tree
We planted
For him

o °o °
  °o

Do the tears
 we shed
    fall
as   rain
   in
 heaven
  ° °
 ° °

Do the flowers
we leave
bloom
in
your ground

are you moving slower than usual?

What's this now?
My legs won't move forward
They feel legitimately restricted
But I just said this has never happened to me
I just filled out that therapy questionnaire
So why do I feel like I'm trenching through
Three hundred tins of golden syrup
Yet my kids are running off
And no matter how fast I go
I'm still stuck behind
I used to run; I used to leg it
So why can't my legs keep up
Why are big strides
Beyond me

breathe in, breathe out

How do I calm down
Breathe. Keep breathing
Why can't I just let go
Uptight. Too tight
Living clung to the edge
Ear ringing
Lip biting
Head hurting
A vigilance so constant
My breath catches in
Shallow cycles
Is there a way to choose
Not to be like this
Go limp
Breath deeper than the ocean
Feel a calmness more
Placid than still waters
Can I go there
Can this be life
Just now
Not then
Not to come
Just breathing in
The gentle air

missing instructions

Why does grief uncover things
You thought you'd left hidden
Why does it make you want to change
Everything and nothing
Why does it separate you
Into pieces
And not leave the instructions
On how to rebuild
Like flat pack furniture
There's always a piece

Missing

the house of catastrophe

No minor inconvenience
Only catastrophe
Lives here
Only worst cases
Are furnished
In this house
There is no talking me down
I'm ready for the tidal wave
There's no calm
After the downpour
Just the grumble
Of thunder

the magic of the morning

Breaking morning
Rich blue sea
Light blue sky
Before the world is awake
The stillness and calm
Little wisps of magic
Dance through the air
A hint of a chill
With the promise of warmth
Arriving
With your echo

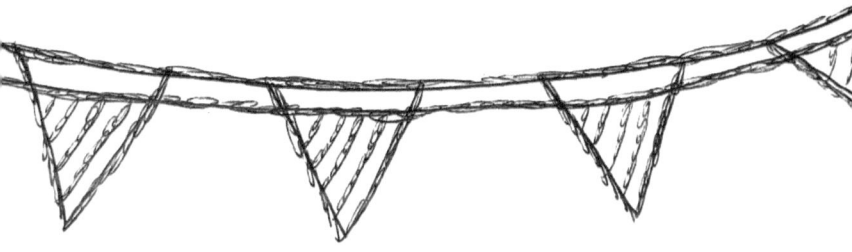

cuddle up, cwtch down

Can I stay at rest
While the rain pours
And the wind whips up
Anything in its path
Can I cuddle up
Cwtch down
Wrap myself
In a blanket of
Everything can wait

Can I wait for this storm
In my mind to pass
With raindrop-covered windows
As my backdrop
And bunting billowing over
The railings
I would like to feel stronger
To face the day
Today

deep foundations

I can't get over
That a big building once stood
Here
A huge feat of concrete
And asbestos
A temporary marvel
Of an industrious age
Bulging over the sea
Plumes covering the sand
It's no longer there
So why can I feel its foundations
Cut into the earth
Leaving only bricks and pipes
Embedded into the sea rocks
The waves eroding
All the memories
But releasing the dust

I can almost see it in the distance
Three chimneys marking its presence
I can feel it appear from nowhere
Springing out from the ground
When walking on the sand
The Earth shudders, rocks give way
To a giant, appearing
Oppressive to the point of sheer power
How can something be gone
But still linger
Still harbour energy
Deeply

flow with me

I don't think there are any words at the minute in this flow
Just the humming of experiences and fears
Reverberating through my memory, unsure where to go
Just the heavy numbness of a shaking arm
held in the air too long
The tedium of a repeating note in a less than perfect song
Of a weight so heavy I feel my feet sinking
into the ground below
The true face of a myriad of feelings and hurts
that I'm unwilling to show
Bouncing between walls and places
grasping more and more to belong
Wanting everyone's opinions to just be silly and wrong
The desire to heal, to climb up from this hefty enduring low
To stop muddling along and to really

Grow

busy bees

Pouring out
A pot of tea
Softly splashing drips and drops
These little puddles
Helping water
The flowers
The pitter patter of
Tiny bees
Helping life sustain
And grow
Tiny drops
Tiny feet
There's no impact
They cannot reach

grief gardening

Who knew grief gardening
Would be a thing
For me
The woman who paved over
The lawn at the last house
We lived in
Every time she bought a plant
It just died
The woman who stated
She disliked gardens so much
That she'd happily live in a flat

So why, as soon as he died
Did a fundamental change
Take place
At my core
My aching, broken core
The weary want of soil and seeds and plants
The dig, the focus, the watching
So much watching
A small seed growing into a towering sunflower
Flowers taking to the soil
Throwing their blooms
Around like confetti

A silver birch swinging its branches
In the breeze I can't see
The hole I dug
Through sunny sweat
To plant it deep
Kneeling on the spider strewn grass
The wildflower seeds we scattered
Spilling over their pots
With reckless growth
It makes me feel something
Inside
A delight in helping
New life

warm the ground

It's half a year since
You were taken away
So I went and bought
Sunflowers and roses
To bless your grave
To say we keep including you
In our life
To burst colour and delight over
Your little body
Under the soil
Orange and pink and yellow and peach and purpley-blue
And stalk green
Resting on dried ground
Just waiting for rain
Thirsty in its drenched desire
The months tear at me
It hurts like an unhealable ache
I feel lost inside a world
That seems to have
Got back on the bus
So flowers in their brilliance
In their radiance, their vibrancy
Will warm the ground
And send my love
Into your soul

swirling and twirling

Will you sit with me
And swirl
Headfirst into the juxtaposition
Of big beautiful love
And the lowest low
Of pain and disbelief
Will you hold my hand
As we merge with
The swirl
Where all emotions come
To dance
Like a spinning top
To a song I don't know the words to

photo album of videos

The thing about Live Photos
Is that they're a very short video
So even if it's not your intention
You've recorded a little film
Each time you click
So every photo we have of him
Is more than just a photo
It's a captured second or so
Of his life

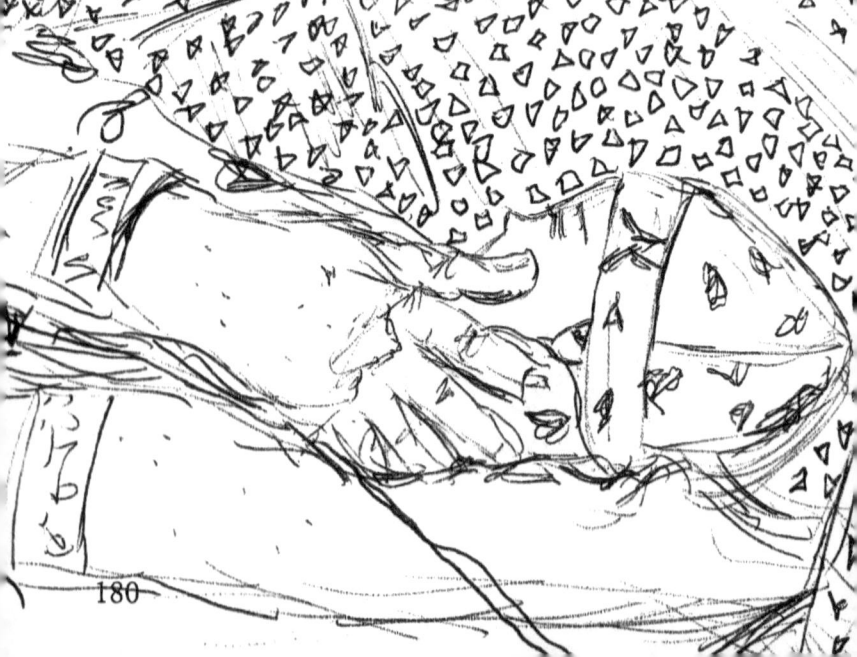

Where my whole body catches
Its breath
When I hold my finger down
And hear his idyllic baby noise
A little murmur
Which I have to ration out
Or I would spend my life
With my finger pressed down
On his face
To hear the gentle noise
Of his life

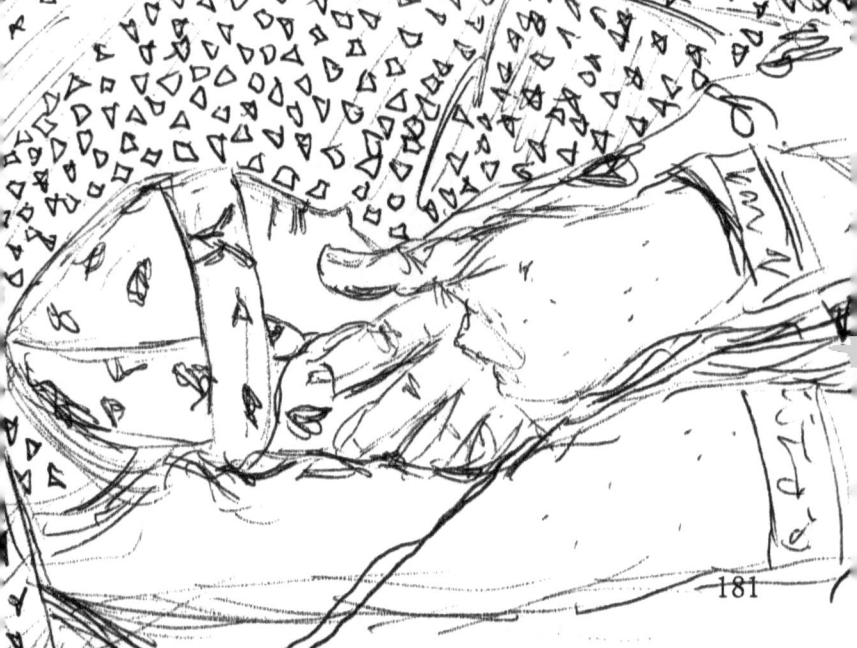

the magic

Can we scream
Out loud
Because we are
Bouncing around
In love
In blessings
In sheer bloody magic

The magic of them
The magic of you

build up break down

Sometimes I feel like
Something's shifted
But then
I'm right back
In hopelessness
In fear
I have a sneaking suspicion
That this might be it now
How it is
Soaring
And shrinking
Building up
And breaking down

heaven

Granny would you hold him close
For me
Tell him how much I love him
Because oh gosh
We miss him
And I miss you too
I know you're living your deaths
In bursts of colour
A miraculous energy
So vibrant it would call us
Home

I don't pretend to know
What heaven looks like
But I think I can identify
A feeling
Only a flicker on Earth
But a flicker of utter calm, utter peace
Utter love
Where everything is better than okay
And the heaviness of being human
Is gone

I know my father-in-law is there too
I know my baby boy is being spoiled
With love
Dancing amongst the stardust
Bathed in beautiful glowing light
Radiant in perfection
Like a magic we can't even dream of
Like a world we cannot even design

Is he growing up
Or eternally just less than
An hour old
Do you talk
Do you eat
Do you do anything we do here
If we are made in His image
Then we must look the same
You see my brain
Just can't make sense of anything
But some things I just know to be
True

I know love doesn't end
Even at death
I know life on Earth
Hurts
And where you are, hurt is but
A whisper on the beat of an angel's wing
And to dust we shall return

But I just want to know
You're okay
Because I'm not
Without you
Can we open the curtains
Just for a second
Just so I can be sure
So I can breathe you in
And let the sparks send shockwaves
Through
Promise me you'll be waiting for me
When I take my final breath

I know you're being enveloped
By your great grandparents, your grandpa
And goodness knows who else
I know you're all there, just beyond
a thin veil
One that sways with the breeze
That catches between realms
One that sends words on the wind
Even when I second guess myself
And stop believing, stop seeing
I still can't stop feeling

But oh I wish
I so dearly, dearly wish
And I don't care how selfish my wishes are
We could change time
Go back and restart
And instead of beautiful heaven
Surrounded by those who have gone before
You were with me here
Being held by me
Instead

take my breath

Sitting here just looking
At the back of the tapestry
Wondering how anything can ever
Make sense
Or be light
Again
I can't see the front
I just see the loose threads
In my homeless world
Where I just can't find a place
To belong
Just loose threads
Hanging down
The beauty lost
For the chaos
And the catastrophe

But someone
Somewhere
Sees the front
Knows the good
And it might just be you
Looking at the intricate beauty
Which would blow my little mind apart
So leave me clinging to the dangling threads
Like hope falling
And one day I'll join you
Home
And I'll hold your hand
As the front of the tapestry takes my breath
And the sense makes itself

alive in the echo

I always said God wouldn't give me another baby
If it wasn't safe
If it wouldn't be okay
But God made me no such promise
I promised for God

But I wouldn't change it
I wouldn't go back and make a different decision
I would do everything exactly the same
It was a gift to be given his
Small life

A rainbow only shows for a short while
But I would rather see it for five minutes
Than never, if I can't see it forever
A flower only blooms for a season
But I would rather see that flower for a while
Than never plant it at all

Some gifts aren't meant to be with us
For long
And through blinding, tearing pain
We are forced to let go
Watch the colours fade
And the petals blow away

Reaching out into the breeze
Hand grasping in desperation
To watch the love fill the world
In all its majesty
Alive in his echo
And the blessed mark he left
On the world

everything for him

My darling
In truth
The kind that is felt way down in the Earth's soil
In the roots of knowing
In startlingly beautiful
Radiant
Truth
We grow it all
For you

Every flower
Every smile
Every night's sleep
Every cry
Every wintry walk
Every gold star
Every fireplace blazing
Every Sunday dinner
Every muddy boot

I hope you feel it
I hope you see it
All
Completely incomplete
Intrinsically inefficient
But the only gifts
We can offer
Are moments
We can live
For you

Love

I don't know
what love is
I only
feel it

with the leaves

All the leaves
Have blown off the big tree
In midsummer
It feels like autumn has
Entered the room
And before I can even catch
My breath
It'll be October
And we'll be at that bloody pumpkin patch
Again
And I'll be holding the pumpkin for you
With the wishful dreams of your growing life
Blown away before
The leaves from the big tree

buoyant anchor

As the crow flies
I can see for miles
Distant and near beaches
Sandwiching blue ocean
Green trees in their summer grandeur
Fields in their browning days
A lighthouse disused in its
Punctuation
Still marking what's gone
Before
Something flickering red
Caught by the early morning light
Like a smouldering ember
Bright yet diminishing
Amidst houses and houses
People with their stories
Floating across life
Any anchor lost
No plunge of galvanised steel
But alive
So alive

akin

It's quiet here in the space between
The breeze through the tree leaves, in early morning
Loud in the roar of the owl's talons
Piecing into tree branches, in the dark
Sending little shards into the ground
Into the earth
Imbibed with the feeling
Of jumbled screams and quiet **numbness**
Of feelings that cannot be restored
Of anger
And of fear
But the earth doesn't panic
It just uses it all
Recycles it
Turns it all round
Until all we can see
Is the beauty of
Everything
Simply nurturing new growth
And nothing is lost
In the air, in water, in the earth
In the blazing fire through
Our minds, our bodies, our souls
For we are all
Akin
Even in the envy, the fright, the depths
We are all
Meant to be

all over the place

Please don't excuse me
Just pretend I'm not here
I'll just be over there
Silently fuming
Feeling a jumble of feelings
Churning up like thick
Sticky butter
Is it jealousy
Is it fear
Is it annoyance
Is it just I'm feeling something
I cannot put words to
A feeling that's an ongoing internal shout
Saying

This is not fair
This is not right
That should be me
Free from the weight
Of deep, deep sadness
I don't want life like this
I feel missing, a lacking
Something and nothing
And everything
A life lived
A life shared
A life I should be breathing into
A life that's fallen
Through my fingers

unrelenting

Is that you breathing fire
In the dark
A ruminating breath of orange and red
With the hum buzz of the night-time
Nightlife
A clang of glass
Empties
Milky white
Brewery dregs
One smash
Many shards
Desperate to roar
into flight

Is that you sweeping through
The midday light
Intermingled
Old empty packets of Haribo
Faded in their reluctance
White weathers
Pristinely clean
Picked petals
Defiant in their droop
Desperate to run
For all your might

Is that you bumbling over
The early morning
When the dew leaves
Its fairy sparkles
On all the green
With the cat
Eager to come in
Scratches
Its yarn down
And down
Desperate with hunger
Fullness in the fight

Is that you yawning through
The afternoon slump
Evening approaches
With its second wind
Crumbled up wrappers
Scrambled in hedgerows
We're not just sitting here
To scare off the crows
Inky in no pretence
Desperate with wanting
In this
Unrelenting plight

looking forward while looking back

It's still summer, just about, but
I feel the call of December
Drawing me in
Skipping past my next birthday
And landing straight
Into advent

Into the countdown
To a birth
To the brightest of all stars
Into the celebration of a baby
Born over two thousand years ago
Who came to change everything

The cold days
The frosty nights
No snow will grace our window panes
But rain will drive home
A feeling of warmth
Because we'll huddle up

We will watch films we've watched
Numerous times
But they'll hit a little harder now
I don't think I can watch the boy wake
To find the snowman gone
Again

I don't think I can wrap a present
Or hang a decoration
Without the gut wrenching
Knowledge of a clear cut piece missing
A visible absence
Strewn through all things

Heart and mind busy with should
He should be almost 1, 2, 3 now
He should be living, breathing, dazzled
With twinkling lights
Dizzy with excitement, with magic
Of a time of year that bursts with hope

Every year we will hang a stocking
With his name
We will think a thousand thoughts
Staring at a tree of multi-colours
Ever-present and ever-feeling
Because he is with us

He is part of the magic
That flows through
Such candle lighting
Vegetable chopping
Big enveloping cuddling
Days

allude me

Swim with the waves
Go with the grain
Hold on to the hand that's offered
Because strength alludes you
Cry a zillions tears
Clean out your insides
Let the tears and rain combine
Make peace with life around you
Let peals of laughter rush on by
Accept, breathe, carry yourself home
Make a coffee and sit with your thoughts
Let them flow and ebb away
Shake them off into the muggy air
Help me with the next malady
Let me drift from side to side
Where is enough
And how do I get there?
Let me bathe in the moon's light
Let me arise with the morning's adoration
Let me delight
                In you

incorrect views

The sky
Cloudless and baby blue
The grass
Overgrown and dewy green
Constants
Like the sea
Like the horizon
Like the harbour
The church spire
Constants in this ever-changing world
Where people come and go
And those left behind
Stare at unchanging emblems
Here before
and long after

But I looked at these views
With different eyes
Before
With an innocence I can't replicate
With a trust in the goodness of life
That I can't conjure up
Anymore

Because everything is coloured differently
And changed
By that liminality
Where my eyes watched
Life leave my newborn baby
Watched breath falter
And a heart stop

And now they can't see anything
In the same way as before
The edges will always be blurring
Ready to unravel with only gentle pulling
But also eager to find the other
That hides in the corners
Of the view
Watched by
Different eyes

life in the lightning bolt

Batten down the hatches
I'm here for the long run
I'm settled in for the crackle of thunder
If a rainbow is the only way
To truly heal
I might be living in a rain cloud
From now on
Living in the lightning bolt
Mesmerised by the raindrops
The vicious wind whipping
Around my shivering spine
Not everyone gets a rainbow
So we can learn to love
Life in the river that threatens
To burst its banks
Rainbows don't wipe
The slate clean
They don't make
Everything suddenly okay

New life and departed life
Live side by side
In the moment
Where the rain still falls
But the sun starts to peek
Through the clouds
And back and forth bounces
The duality of heartbreak
And happiness
But if I just live where
the river bursts its banks
And the thunder booms
And the rain crashes
While the lighting flashes
Finding peace in this new existence
Is okay
As storms have beauty
too

second guessing

What will I do on New Year's Eve
How will I ring in the new year
With faithful gladness
A shaky hand holding a bubbly glass
Praising God
That this woeful year is over
Singing at the top of my lungs to
Bring the next twelve months close as the bell clangs
And clangs
With a joyful damaged heart
That believes there is good to come
Good in the world
Full from the exquisite sadness and bliss
Of Christmas, and a baby being born to
Save the world
Or will I stop it getting its foot in the door
Clasping the old year
Have it prised from my grasping fingers

Because I don't want a year
Where he hasn't drawn breath
I can't face a new year
If it means leaving his life behind
In the old
A year that won't be graced with his beating heart
So perhaps with two hands in opposite directions
I'll finally be torn
Apart
The final threads will be cut
And my pieces will cling to the final clang
In that tower
Clasping with gritted teeth
Until the bell decides
To shake me off and
evict me

grow

I've picked you
    some flowers
        he says
            because
                I love you

Handing me
    several
        flower heads
            that I grew
                myself

Months of
    care
        over
            snatched
                from roots

Blooms wilt
>	in my
>		outstretched
>			hand

Oh, how
>	nice
>		I say

But please,
>	leave the
>		rest
>			to
>				g r o w

where grief goes

If it's possible to feel
Okay and not okay
Together
Then that's where I am

If it's possible to want
To think about you
All the time
But avoid anything deep
Then that's where I lie

If it's possible to talk
About you incessantly
But stop speaking otherwise
Then I might just shut up shop here

If it's possible to look
At just a couple of select photos
And not look at the rest, until tomorrow when I'll
Obsessively look at them all
Then I might just do that for now

If it's possible to be
On a path tied up
In an untyable knot
Then I will be there

If it's possible to want
To seek solitude
But be desperate for company
Then I live in this feeling

If it's possible to desire to
tell your story
And want silence
Together
Then I will pull up a chair here

If it's possible to be lost
In a transient maze
Where up is down
And down is sideways
Then I'll make my home here

If it's possible to steal
Away at the goodness of memories
And critique each one with a heavy hand
Then I know this place

If it's possible to change
My mind again
Feel one way
Then spin on my flat heels
Deciding decisions were okay
Then regretting
Then blaming
Aligned with the unstoppable need to spin

Then
Where grief goes...
I must follow

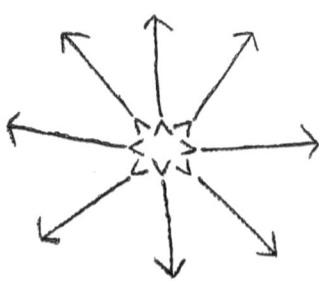

graveside flowers

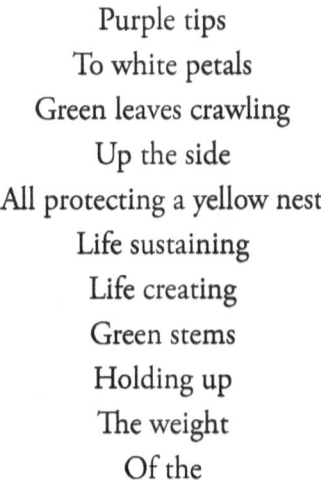

Purple tips
To white petals
Green leaves crawling
Up the side
All protecting a yellow nest
Life sustaining
Life creating
Green stems
Holding up
The weight
Of the
World

look on the bright side?

It's hard to feel grateful
When something terrible has happened
Difficult to count your blessings
When all you feel is the lowest of lows
Impossible to look on the bright side
When the light switch is out of reach
Foolish to dream of better days
When you've seen the worst unfold

Does our
candle light
send sparks
to
your sky

hum a different tune

Can we lose ourselves
In a beautiful moment
Enveloped in a song
So inspiring
You only hear it
Once

Can we fly through
The air
Hitch a ride
With a bird
Grasping onto its
Feathers

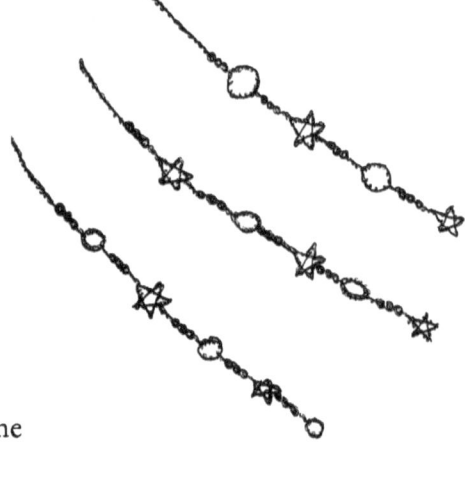

Can we live in an
Image
A small capture of time
Beautiful in beeping
Where completeness was
Real

Can we spin with
The windmill
Dizzy with feeling
Uncontrollable
Exhausted and unable to
Stop

Can we find ourselves
On a quiet rainy
Morning
Humming the same tune
As we busy ourselves with
Living

Can we grow with
The grass
Green and unrelenting
Propagating the memory of
Your life
Everywhere

pour

Let's go round and round
What's this feeling
Floating away
Through my insides
Trying to find a way
Out of this cage
A prison for thoughts
A locked door for rising words
What day is ahead of us
Today
Breathe deep, swallow down
This tricky feeling
Moving up my insides
Go back to sleep
Until another day
Or expelled with a gut wrenching howl
If it's alright with you
I'll just whisper how I feel
To no one in the room

Just to the dust that gathers in the corners
Allow the words to float
Through the kitchen
And set up shop in my teacups
I'll forget those words are there
Until the kettle boils and I
P o u r
Swirl it all around with a
Half-cocked smile
Poised to drink it all
Back down

acrid bliss

Sitting together but sitting alone
A coffee cup just after dawn
As the weather turns slowly
From summer to autumn
In that in between, pre-solstice
Ready to watch the windmill spin
Ready for the cold to seep in
Acrid bliss, the stronger the better

Reflections in rainwater
Laid out on composite decking
That motionless windmill
Seen from every angle
The bird chirping, saying it's mourning
I can't count the clouds
But I know they're indoors too
I can feel their movements

I can feel their weight
But I'm ready for the downpour
I'm willing the blue to turn grey
I'm listening for the birdsong
To tell me something new
I know there's about to be
An onslaught of newness
A gallimaufry of other ways in which

I miss you

ghosts

Rainy afternoon tasks
Make me notice
There's always something new
Always some new flood of grief
Like sticking name labels
On their stuff
Ready for going back to school

Holding three sets of name stickers
In my fumbling hands
He'll never have his name like this
Never have to prove ownership
Never hear his name called out
My insides sink
To the floor

Buying three things
But wanting to pick up four
Three lunch boxes, three bags
Three sets of everything
Ghost objects sitting next to them
A life that should have continued
Extra things that should be cluttering up
The hall

I visualise his name
Black letters, white sticker
I can see it in my mind
But that's all it'll ever be
Ghost words, ghost objects
No one else sees
The only place they live is
Within me

lots of lots of lots

What dawn breaks
after this night's sleep
Do worlds diverge
Before
After
Time.
You've got lots of time now
Lots of quiet
Lots of peace
I don't want peace
I don't want quiet
If I wanted that I wouldn't have wanted
Another baby
I've had peace and quiet
It came with a longing
It came with a price

Years of tests and treatment and time
Lots of time
So I don't want peace
I don't want quiet
I want the cry
I want the shout
I want the billows of laughter
I want life

Dawn breaks
but what awaits
Newness
so much newness

many and none

Can I cover you in a
Bubble mixture
Right as rain
Safe from worst case scenarios
Safe from unexpected storms

When I drive you up to the school gates
Heart heaving with all kinds
Of confusion
If I keep you home with me
Will that fix the ache

When I drive away without
You three, as you clatter crash
Into your school day
I'll cry for him as well as you
Him for having no school days
You for having many

breeze blown

Life has changed irreparably
The future that lay before me
Teemingly turned all the tables
What was to be, now is not
And I am here, still here
Full of life's breath
Full of heart's beat
Tip-toeing through the toadstools
My fairy wings left waiting
For I cannot fly forlorn
Building a new day-to-day dalliance
Caretaker, caregiver, carewisher
Battered, broken and bothered inside
Building up strength morsel by titbit
To face the continually moving escalator
With you, with your cells, in my heart
And the resonance of your life
Thrown into the breeze blown sky
To meet me where I stand

when the queen died

Mum, make sure
The doors
And windows
Are closed
Tonight

I don't want the wind
To take me
To heaven

guarded

What are the chances
That this
Is all
Just a trick of the light

How many tears
Can there
Be here
It's not quite yet night

How many repeats
Of this
Unimaginable pain
Will I carry in this ceremonial rite

How much love will
Flow through
This life
Guarded by winter's icy bite

grasping

Can you grasp the enormity
Of this?
Because I'm not sure I can
We buried acorns
In plastic green pots
To bring the forest home
Because now I've seen death
I only want to see life
I only want to see green
I only want to see his life
Everywhere

Some days I shove down memories
Really deeply
In my mind, in my heart, in my gut
Because it breaks you that little bit more
Every day, to live with death
To replay. To resee
To watch the wildflowers
Lose their colour
To greyness in the ground

To feel the wind moving up
Your spine
An unstoppable force
Something you can't put behind
For thunder crash
For lighting shine
What is this world
Without your smile
Without your laugh
Without your time
Can we pause and just
Rewind

More numerous than the grass blades
More bulbous than the sky clouds
More aching than rotting tree branches
These thoughts. These hurts. These desperate
Desperate words
Can I make sense of
The enormity of this?

Can love break through every
Pavement crack
Every fabric tear
And fill every break
In every damaged heart

in another world

If I dive in
To this sun reflecting
Puddle
Will I emerge
In another world
Glistening and life-filled
Where all flowers
Still bloom
Prudently wild
Stars never misalign
With sparkling shadows
Where raindrops
Fall
Like blithesome laughter
Like a dog shaking
Sending icy drops everywhere
And all rivers
The bluest and deepest
Of rivers
Still flow
And you grow
You grow
Another life just a terrible thought
Shook off
A myriad of thoughts
That nobody here needs to know

weeding

I'm bringing home grass and mud from the cemetery
Stuck around the soles of my boots
I'm bringing home soil in my fingernails
From the wet grass and dewy weeds
I wrenched from the earth
Squatting down in the greenest of grasses
To place yellow roses in a small pot
With the morning dew covering my hands
Like puddle drops of earthy rain
Drunk through the cracks of my rough exterior
Blissful in solitude, core breaking solitude
Living more than one moment
Of floating cloud in blue sky
Of wooden cross
Of hard, hard stone
Of robin's song and crow's caw
Mind full of white coffin, impacted soil
Heart full of soul thoughts, radiant beauty
And boots still half-stuck with browning grass days later
Dropping little whispers of you
Wherever I go

underdeveloped

I don't know how
Today
I don't know why
Today
But my world is full of flashes
Little moments
Captured
Wanting desperately to bring out their images
In a tray of chemicals
Today feels like I'm living a loop
Of disaster
Of crumbling
Utter disaster
Where all I can do
Is look around for you

But there's nothing there
No objects
Only figments
That drift in and out
Of my mind
Of my trick of the light vision
Where I snatch a glimpse
Of a world that never developed
Like 35mm film
In a dark room
Where someone opened a door too soon
Lost with no hope of emergence
Just figments of memory
Of potential, underdeveloped
Drifting
Slowly, so slowly
And gone in an instant
While I desperately try to take another picture

multi-coloured stars

I'm going to
hold

in my hands
a collection

of multi-coloured
stars

then I'll throw
them

into the sky
and watch

as they fall
into the sea

and the trees
and the soil
and the motorway
and the church spire
and the single track road
and the sun bleached fence

and I'll watch
birds

carry them in
their beaks

when the trees
shed their leaves

and they'll feed
their young
tummies full with light

and the sea
will let you float
ready to save

the roads will brush
to the sides
ready for hope
to spring into peripheral vision

and fence panels and soil and spire
will use you
as decoration

to say

goodness

look how beautiful

you are

would you come to stay?

I invited the sea to come and stay
Said you can leave your shells
Under the silver birch tree in the garden
Your sand can stay
Under the decking
But the waves can come indoors
To crash round each room
Rise high, sink low
Flow through the landing
Barge down the stairs
You can stay as long as you like
I will float, buoyantly
Allow you to pull me back and
And push me forwards

Some days you'll be millpond calm
Captivating in your jewel hue
Other days like an uncontrollable demon
Tearing down everything
In your way
Stormy grey in your raggedy riot
But don't think you have to leave just yet
You've not yet outstayed your welcome
I'm learning to live with you, dear waves
Living life in the sea spray

help me know

Lying in the lilac shrubs
Roughage under bare arms
Fingers tangled in greenery
Don't think too much about the crawling
Just look up at petals falling

I'm not going to pick you
I'm going to let you grow
Though my body has flattened
Your growth, it won't stop you
I know

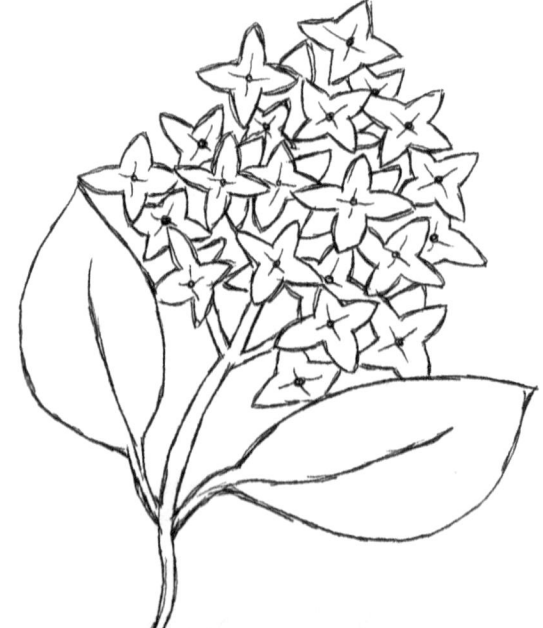

The grass, the clover
The wild wild flowers
Underneath my spine
You flow
I will stay here until I'm ready
To go

I need you, you don't need me
You need the elements
The rain, the shine, the glow
But I gaze to you, I cling to you
I want you to help me know

two sides of the same coin

Flip a coin into the air
Watch it spin
Watch it slow
As it drops

D
 o
  w
   n

D
 o
  w
   n

With a gentle thump
Onto the muddy path
Lying amongst the leaves

One side is
        g r i e f

The other side is
        l o v e

leaf-strewn

Would you like to walk this leaf-strewn path tonight
To relive, to revisit, to exorcise your plight
You see the last time you were here
You carried life within you
Now your feet touch the same gravel
But you walk it anew
On your shoulders you carry death
With memory, with association
With this intake of breath

Exhaling out any pain, any blame
Any hardened feeling hidden in edges
Thoughts of nothing ever, ever being the same
But with this in mind I promise, I'll pledge
To take your ghost hand in mine
And take you to stomp over all the leaves
To listen to the birds tell us it's ok, it's a sign
Because things are at work here we cannot see
In the wind, in the sky, in the swaying pine tree

red-bricked

Would you like to rest
Would you like to numb
Would you like to run

Perhaps just sit
On this side of the glass
To watch as life rolls on

You might find
Your hand creeps
Up the pane

Like longing
Like a need
Like a writhing moment

Because you want life
You feel it inside, hiding round corners
But fear-filled words surround you

You laid these stones
Red-bricked and sturdy
It's safer where the cement has dried

Can you feel the draft
Can you see the sunlight
Can you walk away

If you hold
Your hand out
Will joy be placed

Shall you tear it
All down, risk and panic
Feel it all rise from caverns inside

Would you like to refresh
Would you like to reach
Would you like to go

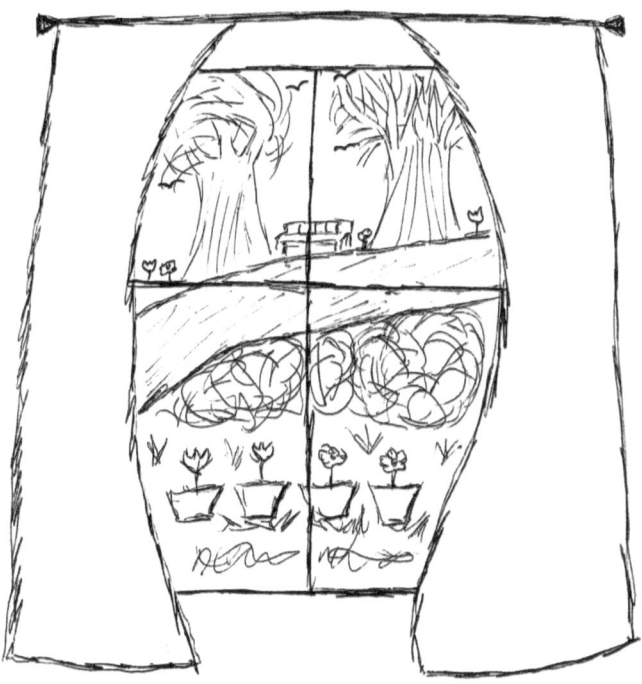

haunting lilt

The images, the minutes, the flow
The sun sprinkled over a buttercup field
The rain dripping down a grass blade
The moon's reflections in your tears
The rumble of the most gargantuan thunder
The haunting lilt of the unheard laugh
The quiet cry through things unseen
Still stuck in a moment, so crisp, so cracked
The moments, the memories, the show
The buttercups picked and thrown
The rain drenching all our clothes
The reflections in windows, in words, in rivers
The heart rumbling with unimaginable pain
The world haunted by a life unfulfilled
The crying quietly in an existence of grief
Still wishing and wanting, so incomplete, so hijacked

raindrops of echoes

Happy birthday to me
The rain blesses me today
I'm lucky, you see
I've had 39 of these so far
Blowing out candles
Gorging on buttercream icing
And the softest sponge
But this year is not how I pictured it
Last year I sat pregnant, posing
With a cake
Thinking, next year you'll be fist grabbing
For a slice of your own
While the rain pours today
It floods with the memories of before
When I believed you'd be here
Now it's just the raindrops of echoes
That draw you near

paper skeletons

Dressing your house up in advance
Like Christmas lights, creeping earlier
Every year
But it's orange. But it's black
Plastic gravestones
And paper skeletons
I'm watching you hold your hands
In the air and make a ghost noise
Skimming the surface is tat
And that gravestone is hollow
Paper skeletons tearing
Limb from limb
From the weight of the wind
Just a bit of fun

Meanwhile my hands are soil-covered
From begging my child
To rise from the dead
To hold a pumpkin on Earth instead
To light the candle with him, not for him
Praying for a sign
For the veil to push back
For a single second
To see, to know, to feel
The other side

The leaves are everywhere
Huddled in piles
Rosy red in delicious defiance
Blowing across the road, the field, the shop doorway
Clinging to window panes
Swirling in the wind
Stuck to pavements in the drops of rain
Each one a shadow of the past
Ready to disintegrate
And be reborn

my baby

My sweet little baby
Sure as the sun rises
And the sea swells
My life will be for you

Your beautiful face
So still, so real
From memory arises
Like petals, from flowers' bloom

Your soul, your all
You gave to us
Picked us from a rising tide
To be yours

In my heart, in my words
You will always live
Candlelit and fire warm
Your light transforms

can you see them?

Tonight, coloured lights
Graced the sky
Followed by the boom
Fireworks joining the light
Of the moon

I watched these sparkles
Disburse through the haze
Sending wonder far and near
And I held back tears
Because you weren't here

I hope, my darling
You see these sparks
Where you rise
Little twinkles bursting through
To reach your skies

every beat of my heart

I'm told a time will come
When it won't be
Quite this painful
When I'll have learnt
To carry this grief
Easier
Like a stalk that doesn't snap
With burgeoning flower
Like a weight that's not got any lighter
But I'll get stronger
And be able to carry it better

I don't know when
That time will come
As my shoulders feel exhausted
My legs buckle
It's all so heavy
The blazing hot sun is too much
For me
I burn too easily

But I believe them
The ones that have come before
The ones that know this
Inside and out
I know they wouldn't lie
Like the wind that carries
The leaves through the air
I trust

So I'll just hold on
And wait
For that spring in my step
And a feeling of lightness
That comes from
Doing the work
And time
Precious, aching time
And I'll breathe in
The pitter patter of raindrops
On my head, on the ground

And I'll thank God
With every beat of my heart
That you came to me

could i be better?

Could I fly back in the night
And wake up earlier in my life
To see things differently
To feel things the opposite way
Could I go back with the security of experience
With the knowledge gained through mistakes, without having to make them
So that I could be with you better
So that I could love you better
So that when it came time for him to arrive
Perhaps the better job I'd done with the others
Would change his future
And I would be running around after one more
Now
And I would be better for all of you
And I wouldn't feel like every mistake made me punished, blame-full, faulted, ashamed
As if he died because I'm not good enough
If I could rewrite, re-envision, redo
Could I be better
Could I please
Just fly back
And be

better

biro rainbow

I'm trying to catch up
On a chilly autumn day
Scribbling notes, scratching into paper
As the sun streams in
Highlighting the specks floating through the air
Sending rays through clear plastic and ink
Making rainbows
Breathing light
Dancing on my page as I write
To remind me that wonder still exists
To tell me that you are here
With the specks
                with the rainbows
                              with me

everyday duality

Little feet clip-clapping around
Soles dancing on tiled flooring
Balloons bursting, sending shockwaves
Sending giggles
Music playing, while an adult tries to herd
Cake being eyed up by little faces
Keen to sneak off with a dab of icing
And screaming, and laughter, and jubilation
The joy of being together
To dance, to run, to play
Eyes on the prize, still as a statue
And you smile because your children
Are happy, are excited and it's beautiful
So you smile

Then your gut betrays you
Your mind, your heart are flooded
And tears threaten
Because there's always going to be one missing
From that party, from every day
And that reality powerfully sweeps away
your moment of bliss
While you search the room for deep-breathing air
Trying to focus, trying to calm
And as you switch back to the room
An invisible line drops through your body
One half feels the most special delight
The other breaks with the most devastating sadness
And you shakily breathe in the duality
        learning to live life
                feeling everything
                        at once

for all of them

We walked down to the seafront
To mark an anniversary
We let the raindrops wash our faces
Like God weeping over the memorial
Writing the letters of your name
In the slightly wet sand
So that even when it seems the world cannot recollect
We know the sea will never forget
Like us, it holds on, inhales the letters
And it breathes your memory
Out, with the break of a wave
Sending the sparks of your life

        e   v

            e   r   y

          w   h   e

                r   e

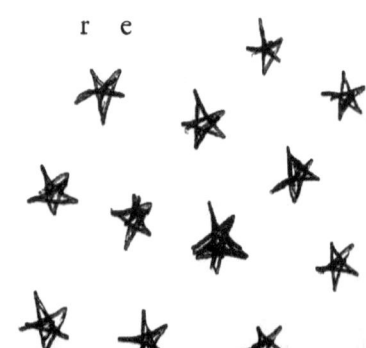

Nine months in...
Nine months out...
Like breathing
In with pregnancy
Out with life
   but
There'll be no comparison photo here
Where burgeoning bump stands
Cushioned by your nine month old
   face
The only photo to show nine months
   out
Is nine months within
   the grave
   the ground
   the stars
   the sky
And arms attached to
   my body
That hold nothing but
   air

about the author & artist

Elizabeth Lockwood lives with her family by the sea. She has three English degrees and a love of books, which led to working in publishing. Elizabeth enjoys coffee (a bit too much), reading, writing, doodling, scenic walks, baking (and eating) cakes, and anything magical.

IG: @stars.and.leaves

about osian

Osian Lockwood was born in January 2022 at 35 weeks. He lived for 53 minutes. Osian had trisomy 18 and an unbalanced translocation of 3 and 21.

He is eternally loved and much missed by his parents, sisters, brother, and family.

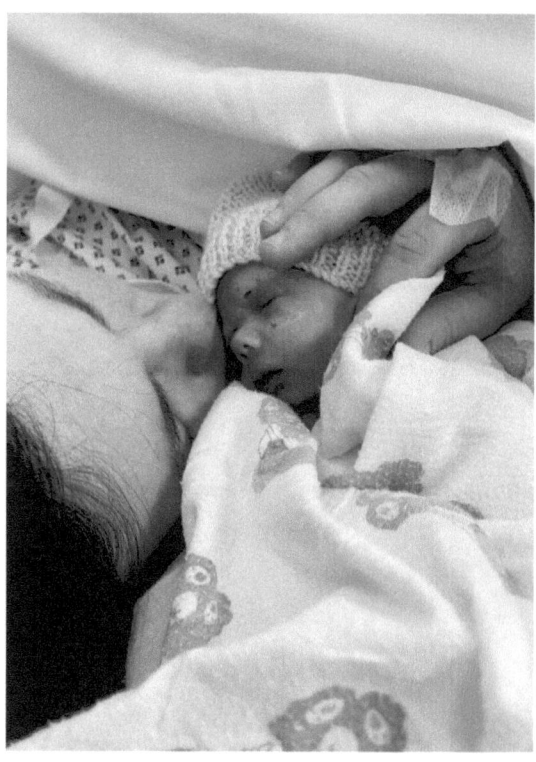

for help:

2Wish
Support for those affected by sudden death
in young people in Wales
www.2wish.org.uk

Soft U.K.
Support Organisation for Trisomy 13/18
www.soft.org.uk

Sands
Stillbirth and neonatal death charity
www.sands.org.uk

Tommy's
Baby loss support and research
www.tommys.org

Aching Arms
Bringing comfort after pregnancy and baby loss
www.achingarms.co.uk

Together for Short Lives
The UK charity for children and young people expected to have short lives
www.togetherforshortlives.org.uk

SiMBA charity
Simpson's memory box appeal
www.simbacharity.org.uk

with gratitude to

Michelle, Lu, Catriona, Paul, Tabitha, Dominic,
Robyn, Osian, my family & friends, 2wish charity,
SiMBA charity, Together for Short Lives
charity, the maternity, bereavement, and
paediatric palliative care departments
of Glangwili Hospital,
Carmarthen

also by turquoise quill press

For every perceived failure, a zillion expanded worlds
Edges become blurry, as all becomes one
Grace is substantial, the rest will fade
Only Love. always Loved
Falling in Love with myself
We are the Heavens in drops of Gold

hope dealer is a book of poetry and illustrations by
Catriona Messenger.

Gifting – an asking – a wanting
To know who we were before
Life excels in teaching
You to walk again
What if it's All a gift
To keep Love breathing
We allow the Divine in pain
Our wonderous collaboration on earth
Not offers of safety, But many offers of Alive

life dealer is the second book of poetry and illustrations by Catriona Messenger.

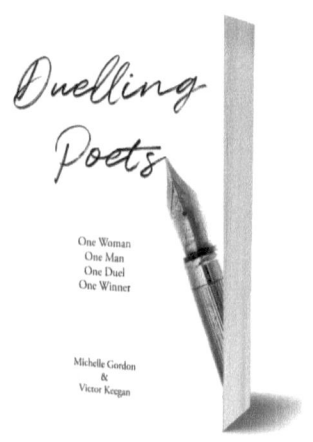

For 30 days in 2012, Michelle and Victor each wrote a poem a day, taking turns to choose the titles. Michelle is an author, who was in her late 20s at the time, and Victor, a retired journalist in his 70s. Their differing experiences and perspectives created contrasting poems, despite being written about the same theme. In Duelling Poets, we invite you to read the poems and choose your favourites, then at the end, you can see which poet wins the duel for you.

Turquoise Quill Press is an imprint of Not From This Planet

NotFromThisPlanet.co.uk

www.ingramcontent.com/pod-product-compliance
Lightning Source LLC
Chambersburg PA
CBHW030034100526
44590CB00011B/196